HOMES IN A BOX
MODERN HOMES FROM SEARS ROEBUCK

Schiffer Publishing Ltd

4880 Lower Valley Road, Atglen, PA 19310 USA

Published by Schiffer Publishing Ltd.
4880 Lower Valley Road
Atglen, PA 19310
Phone: (610) 593-1777; Fax: (610) 593-2002
E-mail: Info@schifferbooks.com
Please visit our web site catalog at
www.schifferbooks.com

This book may be purchased from the publisher.
Include $3.95 for shipping. Please try your bookstore first.
We are always looking for people to write books on new and
related subjects. If you have an idea for a book please contact
us at the above address.
You may write for a free catalog.

In Europe, Schiffer books are distributed by
Bushwood Books
6 Marksbury Avenue
Kew Gardens
Surrey TW9 4JF England
Phone: 44 (0) 20-8392-8585; Fax: 44 (0) 20-8392-9876
E-mail: info@bushwoodbooks.co.uk
Free postage in the UK. Europe: air mail at cost.

ISBN: 0-7643-0432-1
Printed in China

INTRODUCTION

Sears Roebuck-Homes in a Box, is a facsimile reproduction of the Sears *Modern Homes* catalog. It gives a nostalgic look at the more than one hundred home kits sold by Sears Roebuck in the early 1900s. These homes were offered as simple kits with only the blueprints and bill-of-materials or as complete homes with all materials and finishes. By using one step distribution, Sears was able to leverage mass buying power into substantial cost savings for their customers and it all carried Sears' famous money back guarantee.

It's astounding, that by today's standards of direct marketing, Sears was able to offer such a large, diverse group of home designs. The architectural styles ranged from simple bungalows to beautiful homes with a strong Frank Lloyd Wright influence. Much of this Wright influence can be traced to the proliferation of Wright homes in the Chicago area, Sears home base.

If you or your contractor did not want the whole package but were looking for the lowest price on only building materials, Sears could provide lumber and mill work at wholesale prices, they deliver form their saw mills in the south or from their plants and lumber yards in Chicago, direct to your building site. Sears was the complete mail order building supplier, offering catalogs for furnaces, water heaters, hardware, plumbing, concrete blocks, bricks, fireplaces, along with paints, varnishes and finishing materials. All these materials were backed by Sears money back guarantee.

Thousands of these homes are still standing and still providing shelter to families across the country. Many of them are unaware of the source of their home's design. This book will help them trace their architectural heritage. It will also be an invaluable tool to those looking to trace the architectural history of the American home.

Are You Looking for a Home?

THIS book has solved the home building problem for thousands of people. No matter whether you are looking for an imposing residence, a modern bungalow or a cozy cottage you will surely be able to make a suitable choice from the 110 designs illustrated, described and priced in the following pages. If you have made up your mind to break away from the rent paying class this year and join the independent army of home owners you could not possibly have made a better beginning than you have by getting this Book of Modern Homes. You do not have to pay a penny for architectural services. We give you free, plans, specifications and an itemized bill of materials of the kind that would cost you about $100.00 from a local architect. For our offer of free plans see page 3. We furnish materials for the house of your choice, from the foundation to the roof, with the exception of cement, brick and plaster, which we do not furnish. Our materials are guaranteed to be the best of their kind on the market, insuring a permanent building.

The pictures shown above were copied from actual photographs of houses built according to our plans and with our materials. The owners will tell you that we saved them from 25 to 50 per cent and gave them grades of material that they could not possibly duplicate in the local market. (See page 114.)

Stop Paying Rent. Quit Building "Castles in the Air." Build a Real Castle—A Home of Your Own.

If you keep on paying rent for another year you will not be any better equipped to start building than you are at this moment. On the other hand, you will have wasted the whole year's rent, which you ought to have applied on the cost of your own building. Why look around for a new flat or a temporary cottage which you will very probably move away from in six or twelve months' time. Why not have a place where you will have plenty of room for the children to play, where there will be no embarrassing protests from your neighbors in the flat below? You have seen the signs on buildings reading "Tenants with children not desired." Does not this condition of affairs make it necessary for you to make up your own mind NOW that **you will build your own home?** Don't waste your time dreaming of the home you are going to have "sometime." **Build it this year.**

Build Now. We Have the House You Want at the Price You Want to Pay.

If you really want a home, if you want to construct it of first class materials and wish to save at least $500.00 on the job, sit down today and write us for full particulars regarding our building proposition. Remember that money alone never built anything, whereas **Resolution, Grit and Co-operation** have improved entire sections and created big cities. We will show you how to secure the house of your choice if you will simply take the trouble to consult us. First make your selection of a house from this book, then send for plans, specifications and bill of materials, and when you have studied them thoroughly we will be at your service for any particular information you may desire. We have helped thousands of people to become home owners. **Let Us Help You.**

96h.1.1.24.12.30

Your Choice of Over One Hundred Modern Homes

Plans Drawn by Licensed Architects of Wide Experience, Embodying All the Very Newest Ideas in Convenient and Artistic Arrangement

HUNDREDS of our customers during the past year selected homes from former editions of this book, built them or had them built by contract according to our plans and with our materials, and they saved from $500.00 to $1,000.00 each. These big savings have made them our best advertisers. Read the letters from customers on page 114 and see the pictures of their homes on page 115.

We satisfy our customers by furnishing the highest grades of material at lower prices than are asked anywhere else. They all endorse our methods and recommend them to others. While our estimates, including labor, on the houses in this book are considered very low, many of our customers have built according to our plans for even less than our figure. Furthermore, our proposition is different from any other, because we guarantee every dollar's worth of building material we sell. Should we fail to please you, you take no risk; you are at liberty to return all or any part of the material purchased from us which proves unsatisfactory and we will cheerfully return your money and any freight charges you have paid.

Consider carefully the houses shown in this book, study the floor plans of each, and when you find a house that appeals to you write for the plans, specifications and itemized bill of materials in accordance with our offers on page 3. Our plans or blue prints are much more carefully drawn than the plans provided by the average architect who charges from $100.00 to $200.00 for his services, ours being accurate and correct in detail. They are the work of architects of wide experience; the typewritten specifications thoroughly cover the method of constructing the house, insuring a first class job. The bill of materials, which is a part of our plans, but which is never supplied by the average architect, carefully itemizes every foot of lumber, every item of building material of every description; in fact, this bill of materials is our bid. We will agree to furnish all materials for the amount specified in our bill of materials, which amount to the same as the amount specified in the pages of this book for each house.

The cost of the original tracings, the writing of the original specifications and bill of materials for each of the houses in this book is from $100.00 to $200.00, varying according to size and style of the house. From the original tracing sheets we have reproduced a large number of plans and have printed a supply of bills of materials. We are offering them to our customers on a very liberal plan, enabling you to get plans of the very highest class, with specifications and bills of materials which originally cost $100.00 to $200.00, for $1.00 in cash or free of charge, as per our offers on page 3.

Our object in making such a liberal offer to the public is to quickly convince prospective builders that we can make them big savings in building material. While one might possibly overlook the fact that we can make him a saving of a few dollars on any one item, he cannot overlook the fact that we can save him $150.00 to $1,500.00 or more on a building. This Book of Modern Homes puts the matter of our money saving prices so forcibly before the prospective builder that he cannot overlook the great advantages in buying mill work and all building materials from us. Our bill of materials forms a basis for comparison; in fact, it is our bid. You can tell at once just what any part of the building material will cost you, or the whole lot, as you please. It furnishes convincing proof that we can make you a very large saving.

There is no mystery in our prices; they are simply the natural result of our well known policy of merchandising, selling goods at prices based on the actual cost to produce with but one profit added. The application of this principle to mill work, lumber, lath, shingles and other building material—a line on which everybody has been obliged to pay big prices heretofore because of market conditions, monopolies, manufacturers' agreements or local associations made for the purpose of keeping up prices—enables us to make you a large saving, while at the same time we are able to give you absolutely the finest quality throughout. Every item of building material we handle is backed by our unlimited guarantee of satisfaction or money returned.

On pages near the back of this book we show designs for barn plans.

SEARS, ROEBUCK AND CO.   —2—   CHICAGO, ILLINOIS

OFFER No. 1

Complete Set of Plans, Specifications and Bill of Materials for $1.00

As explained on opposite page, the plans, specifications and bill of materials for each of the modern homes in this book were prepared by licensed architects of wide experience at a cost to us of from $100.00 to $200.00 per set. We have gone to considerable expense to reproduce these blue prints from the original tracing sheets by printing and preparing many sets of specifications and bills of materials for our customers, but for the purpose of getting the public acquainted with our wonderful building proposition we are willing to sell outright these complete sets of blue prints, specifications and bills of materials at the small sum of $1.00 a set. This amount must be included with your order. We feel that we can afford to make this liberal offer in view of the convincing proof that these blue prints, specifications and bill of materials contain in regard to the money saving we offer you in building material.

OFFER No. 2

Complete Set of Plans, Specifications and Bill of Materials Free

If you are going to build this year we gladly make you this free offer: Select the home in this book that appeals to you, fill in the accompanying order blank, giving number of plan wanted, and send it to us, together with $1.00 in the form of a money order, or currency, stating that you are thinking of building this year, and we will mail you, postage prepaid, a complete set of these plans, and at the same time will send you a certificate for $1.00 to apply on any order for mill work. We will accept this certificate as $1.00 in cash if accompanied by an order for mill work, such as doors, windows, molding, etc., whether the order is small or large. In this way you get these plans, specifications and bill of materials free of charge.

We Want to Explain Our Object in Making the Two Above Liberal Offers

Considering the original cost of these blue prints, specifications and bill of materials and the cost to reproduce them, you will agree with us that we are making you an exceptionally liberal offer. We have nothing to gain from this alone. The plans of this high character, showing all the details, covering every part of the building operation, the typewritten specifications covering from three to five pages of closely written matter, and the bill of materials which plainly itemizes every kind of material required in the building of any one of these houses and which serves as our bid for the entire building, even though they were duplicated in vast quantities, could not be disposed of profitably according to our offers. Our only object is to convince you that we can save you from $150.00 on a house usually costing $600.00 to build to $1,500.00 on a house usually costing $6,000.00 to build. We want nothing more than the opportunity to place these plans, specifications and bill of materials in the hands of anyone intending to build, or in the hands of any contractor, builder or carpenter, because we know that as they furnish a basis of comparison for qualities and prices with the qualities and prices of material furnished by dealers elsewhere, we will get the orders. Don't let anyone mislead you into believing that our low prices are due to an inferior quality. We guarantee to furnish absolutely the most dependable grades of building material on the market. You are at liberty to return any goods that do not measure up to the standard we claim for them and we will, without question or quibble, return both the price and any transportation charges you paid on them. Take advantage of either of these liberal offers. You cannot fully appreciate the great saving we are able to make you on building materials until you receive a complete set of our plans, specifications and bill of materials, for **they are the proof.** They will convince anyone.

All prices quoted in this book are F. O. B. the cars at our factory or yards.
Lumber is quoted F. O. B. the cars at our yards in Illinois.
Mill work and finish are quoted F. O. B. the cars at our mills in Eastern Iowa.
Hardware, paints and other accessories are quoted F. O. B. the cars at Chicago, Ill.
We will gladly quote you prices delivered to your station on request.

MODERN HOME No. 146

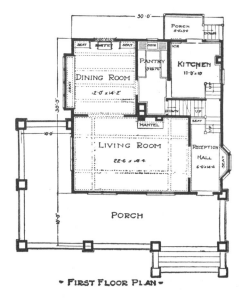

- FIRST FLOOR PLAN -

- SECOND FLOOR PLAN -

On the following pages we show illustrations of the interior of this house, also interior trim, showing the class of material we furnish. Note that our prices are never made at the expense of quality. All our material is guaranteed.

$1,660.00

For $1,660.00 we will furnish all the material to build this Seven-Room Residence, consisting of Lumber, Lath, Shingles, Mill Work, Ceiling, Siding, Flooring, Finishing Lumber, Buffet, Medicine Case, Building Paper, Pipe, Gutter, Sash Weights, Hardware and Painting Material. NO EXTRAS, as we guarantee enough material at the above price to build this house according to our plans.

By allowing a fair price for labor, cement, brick and plaster, which we do not furnish, this house can be built for about $3,960.00, including all material and labor.

For Our Offer of Free Plans See Page 3.

EXTRA large living room with paneled oak beam ceiling, rustic brick fireplace. The doors are veneered oak of the latest Craftsman design with oak trim to match. Large cased openings lead to the reception hall and the dining room. The dining room has paneled oak beam ceiling and modern buffet with seats at each side and large window seats along the windows of the exposed side. Large well lighted reception hall has a bay window and a window seat. This hall leads to an oak open stairway of modern pattern. The unique arrangement of the stairs enables one to reach the second floor from the kitchen or from the reception hall. The cellar stairs are placed directly under the main stairs. The pantry between the dining room and kitchen distinctly separates the kitchen from the rest of the house. A cased opening connects the pantry with the kitchen. The doors, staircase, window seats and interior trim of the first floor are finished in the best quality of oak with clear oak flooring in the reception hall, living room and dining room. The kitchen and pantry floors are made of the best grade of maple.

Note the well arranged second floor plan. Like the rest of the plan, every foot of space is utilized to the very best advantage. Three large airy bedrooms, each with large windows on two sides, giving plenty of light and ventilation, with closets adjoining. Plate glass mirror door in front bedroom. Even the small bedroom or servant's room has light and ventilation from two sides. The entire second floor has selected birch trim with birch six-cross panel doors to match. All flooring on the second floor is made of clear maple. Our architect in planning this house has planned on economy in heating, which can be plainly seen by this economical arrangement.

Clear cypress siding from water table to second story window sills; balance of second story and roof shingled with cedar shingles. Edge grain fir flooring 1⅛ inches thick for porch.

A large roomy veranda with massive stonekote columns. Ornamental Priscilla windows are specified for the attic. Colored leaded art glass over the buffet in the dining room. All windows and doors are of the very latest style.

Foundation is made of concrete block.

Excavated basement under the entire house, 7 feet high from floor to joists. First floor, 9 feet high from floor to ceiling; second floor, 8 feet high from floor to ceiling; attic room, 14x14 feet, 7 feet high from floor to collar beams. Gables and columns are sided with stonekote, the most modern style of construction.

This house can be built on a lot 46 feet wide.

Complete Warm Air Heating Plant, for soft coal, extra	$ 97.37
Complete Warm Air Heating Plant, for hard coal, extra	99.90
Complete Steam Heating Plant, extra	177.44
Complete Hot Water Heating Plant, extra	232.05
Complete Plumbing Outfit, extra	166.30

SEARS, ROEBUCK AND CO.  **CHICAGO, ILLINOIS**

THE INTERIOR OF OUR MODERN HOME No. 146

OUR architects have devoted much careful study and spent considerable time in preparing the plans for all houses illustrated in this catalog. The specifications, working plans and itemized bill of material for every house shown herein have been proven by the experience in erecting, eliminating all guesswork.

On the following pages we show some of the items of building materials which we furnish for this modern home. A comparison of prices will show that we can save you at least one-fourth in the cost of building materials with the use of our plans, as compared with what it would cost you if you purchased your building materials elsewhere and used the usual kind of incomplete plans.

MATERIAL SPECIFIED FOR MODERN HOME №146

Birch Interior Door, 2 feet 8 inches by 7 feet, 1⅜ inches thick. Price...**$3.18**

Craftsman Oak Interior Door, 2 feet 8 inches by 7 feet, 1⅜ inches thick. Price ..**$5.65**

Closet Door for front chamber, birch, 2ft. 6in. x7 ft., with beautiful full length plate glass mirror. Price..**$17.15**

Rear Outside Door, 3x7 feet, 1¾ inches thick, glazed. Price..**$4.80**

Craftsman Oak Front Door, glazed plate glass; 3x7 feet, 1¾ inches thick. Price **$8.25**

Two-Light CheckRail Window, 2 feet by 4 feet 6 inches, with glass. Price.....**71c**

Craftsman Oak Buffet, bevel plate glass mirror, doors glazed with leaded art glass. Price ..**$46.00**

Note our low prices. All our material is guaranteed. We furnish the very latest designs at half regular prices. For complete line see our Building Material Catalog.

All the doors, buffet and other materials shown on this page represent a few of the items we furnish for Modern Home No. 146 shown on page 4.

7⅞ × 5½

Stop

Inside Door Jambs. Yellow pine...**$0.45** Oak..........**.78** Birch........**1.02**

QUALITY GUARANTEED

QUALITY GUARANTEED

MATERIAL SPECIFIED FOR MODERN HOME Nº 146

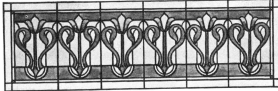

Colored Art Nouveau Leaded Glass over buffet.
Price, per foot.................................$1.65

Craftsman Oak Plate Rail, five members.
Price, per foot......18½c

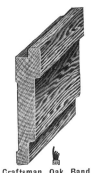

Craftsman Oak Band Picture Mold. Price, per 100 feet.................$3.25

Craftsman Oak Two-Member Casing. Price, per 100 feet..$3.30

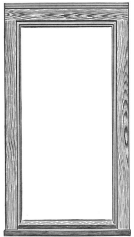

Outside Window Frame, 2 feet by 4 feet 6 inches, with pulleys.
Price $1.62

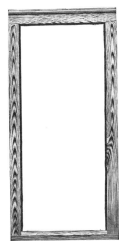

Outside Door Frame, 1⅛-inch outside casing, 1¾-inch thick oak sill. Price......$1.90

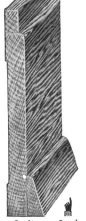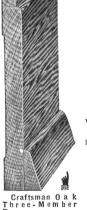

Craftsman Oak Three-Member Base. Price, per 100 feet.......$6.40

Craftsman Oak Window Stool.
Price, per 100 feet......$4.75

Craftsman Oak Window Apron. Price, per 100 feet ...$2.50

Craftsman Oak Picture Molding. Price, per 100 feet........$1.60

Clear Yellow Pine Flooring. ⅞x3¼-inch face.
Price, per 1,000 feet.......$28.60

Clear Oak Flooring, 13-16x 2¼-inch face.
Price, per 1,000 feet....$59.50

We specify the highest class of materials; strictly up to date designs. Our low prices explain why you can build a $5,000.00 house for $3,960.00 when you trade with us.

QUALITY GUARANTEED

Cupboard Door, 1 foot 6 inches by 2 feet 6 inches, 1⅛ inches thick. Price.....56c

The interior of a home finished with materials such as shown on this page is sure to please. There are none better made at any price. We guarantee to please our customers.

QUALITY GUARANTEED

MATERIAL SPECIFIED FOR MODERN HOME № 146

Craftsman Oak Stair Rail, 2½x3½ inches. Price, per lineal foot.............**14c**

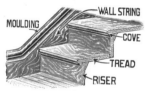

MOULDING — WALL STRING — COVE — TREAD — RISER

OAK STAIRS.
Treads. Price, each.............**49c**
Risers. Price, each.............**22c**
Two-Member String Board. Price, per foot.............**12½c**

Oak Thresholds. Price, each.......**4c**

Front Door Lock Set, solid bronze trimming. Price......**$5.49**

Rear Door Lock Set, solid bronze trimming. Price......**99c**

Oak Stair Newel. Price......**$2.96**

Oak Angle Stair Newel. Price, **$1.81**

Sash Cord. Price, per 100 feet.....**67c**

Yellow Pine Kitchen Base, 7¼ inches high. Price, per 100 feet.........**$2.77**

Three-Member Cap Trim, yellow pine. Price, per 100 feet.........**$4.00**

Three-Member Birch Baseboard, 9½ in. high. Price, per 100 feet.**$7.09**

Yellow Pine Window Stool. Price, per 100 feet....**$2.30**

Yellow Pine Window Stop, ⅜x1⅜ inches. Price, per 100 feet......**33c**

Yellow Pine Window Apron. Price, per 100 feet..**$1.45**

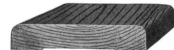

Yellow Pine Casing, 4¼ inches wide. Price, per 100 feet.............**$1.65**

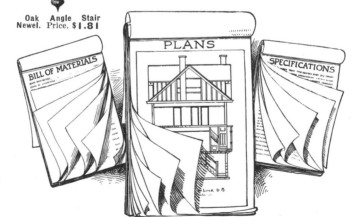

BILL OF MATERIALS

PLANS

SPECIFICATIONS

Plans, Specifications and Bill of Materials which we furnish free as offered on page 3.

Cove Molding. Price, per 100 feet.......**30c**

Outside House Paint, guaranteed. In 5-gallon lots. Price, per gallon....**$1.15**

5 GALLONS READY MIXED HOUSE PAINT

Inside Door Lock Sets, plated bronze trimming. Price, each..........**54c**

Hinges and Screws to match trimming. Price, per pair........**28c**

MODERN HOME No. 158

$1,700.00

For $1,700.00 we will furnish all the material to build this modern Nine-Room Residence, consisting of Lumber, Lath, Shingles, Mill Work, Ceiling, Siding, Flooring, Finishing Lumber, Building Paper, Pipe, Gutter, Sash Weights, Mantel, Hardware and Painting Material. **NO EXTRAS**, as we guarantee enough material at the above price to build this house according to our plans.

By allowing a fair price for labor, cement, brick and plaster, which we do not furnish, this house can be built for about $3,895.00, including all material and labor.

For Our Offer of Free Plans See Page 3.

THE ROOMS in this house are conveniently arranged with a reception hall opening into the dining room on one side and to a very large living room on the other side. The kitchen and pantry are practically separated from the remainder of the house with entrance from the kitchen to the dining room through the pantry. An open staircase leads from the reception hall to the second floor. The second floor contains four large chambers and a large balcony which can be screened in and used as an open air sleeping porch.

The beam ceiling is worked into one design for the living room, hall and dining room, with a mantel at the end of the large living room.

Front and side doors are veneered oak, of the proper design to match the windows. Interior doors for the main rooms on the first floor are six-cross-panel veneered oak, with casing, baseboard, trim and stairs of clear oak. The doors for the kitchen and servant's room are clear yellow pine. The second floor doors are clear birch, six-cross panel, with birch casing, baseboard and trim.

Front door cylinder locks and all interior door locks are genuine bronze, other hardware to match.

This house is of a practically square design and can be built at a very reasonable price.

The pergola, which is 24x10 feet, is a very popular feature in modern homes and in this case being on the opposite side from the kitchen and servant's room makes the house look well balanced.

Pergolas are fast becoming popular. They make a delightful retreat in warm weather. This house has a very roomy porch, 32 feet long by 9 feet wide.

This house is built on a concrete foundation and is of frame construction. The first story is covered with narrow bevel edge cypress siding, the second story with cedar shingles and has a cedar shingle roof.

Painted two coats outside; your choice of color. Varnish and wood filler for two coats of interior finish.

Excavated basement under the entire building, 7 feet high from floor to joists, divided into three rooms; one for laundry, one for storage and the other for heating plant and coal. Rooms on the first floor, 9 feet from floor to ceiling; rooms on the second floor, 9 feet from floor to ceiling. One large room in the attic.

This house can be built on a lot 56 feet wide.

Complete Warm Air Heating Plant, for soft coal, extra	$114.51
Complete Warm Air Heating Plant, for hard coal, extra	117.05
Complete Steam Heating Plant, extra	228.40
Complete Hot Water Heating Plant, extra	281.04
Complete Plumbing Outfit, extra	184.39

SEARS, ROEBUCK AND CO.  **CHICAGO, ILLINOIS**

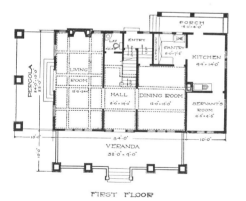

FIRST FLOOR

SECOND FLOOR

MODERN HOME No. 132

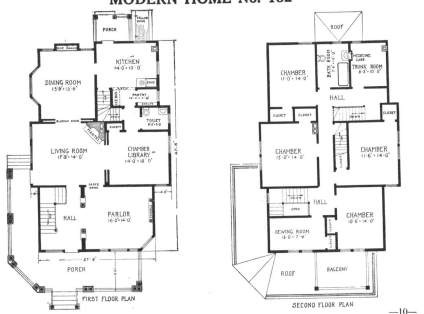

FIRST FLOOR PLAN

SECOND FLOOR PLAN

—10—

$2,170.00

For $2,170.00 we will furnish all the material to build this Twelve-Room House, consisting of Lumber, Lath, Shingles, Mill Work, Flooring, Ceiling, Siding, Finishing Lumber, Building Paper, Pipe, Gutter, Sash Weights, Mantel, Medicine Case, China Closet, Console, Hardware and Painting Material. NO EXTRAS, as we guarantee enough material at the above price to build this house according to our plans.

By allowing a fair price for labor, cement, brick and plaster, which we do not furnish, this house can be built for about $4,480.00, including all material and labor.

For Our Offer of Free Plans See Page 3.

A LARGE, roomy house, well designed and suitable for a corner lot, having large front porch 42x9 feet, and large bay window in the dining room, with an outside door opening from the porch into the living room, front door opens into the reception hall. Large colonnade between the hall and parlor. Well designed oak open stairway. The hall leads to the living room, parlor or second floor. Cased opening between the living room and parlor. Sliding doors between the living room and library; sliding doors between the living room and dining room. China closet or sideboard set into the wall of the dining room. Colored leaded art glass sash on each side of sideboard above plate rail. Rear stairway leading to the second floor from the kitchen with cellar stairs directly underneath. Toilet on the first floor. On the second floor there are four large bedrooms, sewing room, storeroom or trunk room, and bathroom which has medicine case built into the wall.

Two front doors of veneered oak, glazed with bevel plate glass. Two-panel veneered oak inside doors and clear oak casing, baseboard and molding throughout the entire house. Quarter sawed oak flooring for the main rooms on the first floor and clear yellow pine flooring for the second floor and porches. Mantel in living room, and console with large mirror in parlor.

Painted two coats outside. Varnish and wood filler for two coats of interior finish.

Built on a concrete block foundation, frame construction, sided with narrow bevel edge siding of clear cypress and has cedar shingle roof.

Excavated basement under the entire house, 7 feet from floor to joists, with cement floor. First floor, 10 feet from floor to ceiling; second floor, 9 feet from floor to ceiling.

This house can be built on a lot 50 feet wide.

Complete Warm Air Heating Plant, for soft coal, extra	$112.86
Complete Warm Air Heating Plant, for hard coal, extra	115.40
Complete Steam Heating Plant, extra	296.70
Complete Hot Water Heating Plant, extra	346.00
Complete Plumbing Outfit, extra	180.71

SEARS, ROEBUCK AND CO.  CHICAGO, ILLINOIS

MODERN HOME No. 118

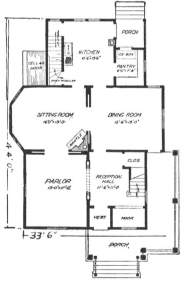

PLAN OF FIRST FLOOR

SECOND FLOOR

$1,477.00

For $1,477.00 we will furnish all the material to build this Nine-Room House, consisting of Lumber, Lath, Shingles, Mill Work, Siding, Flooring, Ceiling, Finishing Lumber, Building Paper, Pipe, Gutter, Sash Weights, Hardware, Mantel and Painting Material. NO EXTRAS, as we guarantee enough material at the above price to build this house according to our plans.

By allowing a fair price for labor, cement, brick and plaster, which we do not furnish, this house can be built for about $3,060.00, including all material and labor.

For Our Offer of Free Plans See Page 3.

MODERN Home No. 118 is a well proportioned house, suitable for any locality. One is immediately impressed on approaching this house by its quiet dignity and comfort. The large, roomy porch, 7 feet wide by 33 feet long, seems to invite one to its cool shade.

Upon entering the reception hall we find to the right a nice open stairway of oak leading to the second floor. At the foot of the stairs there is a little nook which will make a nice cozy corner.

On the first floor there are five large rooms, including the reception hall. The sitting room has a large bay window extending entirely across one side of the room. In the corner of the sitting room is an oak mantel and open fireplace. Leading from the reception hall to parlor is a cased opening with oak columns. Between parlor and living room is placed sliding doors. The kitchen is very handily arranged, having a large pantry. This pantry has a small opening in the back which admits of filling the ice chest from the back porch, doing away with having the ice carried across the kitchen floor.

The second floor has three large bedrooms and a good size bathroom, two of the bedrooms have large closets.

All the rooms on the first floor, excepting the kitchen, are finished in oak with oak flooring and six-cross panel veneered oak doors. Outside doors are of elegant design made of clear oak. Oak plate rail is furnished to go entirely around the dining room. Maple flooring is furnished for the kitchen and pantry. The second floor is finished in yellow pine, solid five-cross panel yellow pine doors. Clear yellow pine flooring for the second floor and porches.

Painted two coats outside. Varnish and wood filler for two coats interior finish.

This house is of frame construction, sided with narrow bevel edge siding and has cedar shingle roof. Built on a concrete block foundation.

Excavated basement under the entire house, 7 feet 4 inches from floor to joists. First floor, 9 feet from floor to ceiling; second floor, 8 feet 6 inches from floor to ceiling.

This house can be built on a lot 38 feet wide.

Complete Warm Air Heating Plant, for soft coal, extra	$103.06
Complete Warm Air Heating Plant, for hard coal, extra	105.11
Complete Steam Heating Plant, extra	219.65
Complete Hot Water Heating Plant, extra	278.08
Complete Plumbing Outfit, extra	124.53

SEARS, ROEBUCK AND CO.  **CHICAGO, ILLINOIS**

MODERN HOME No. 164

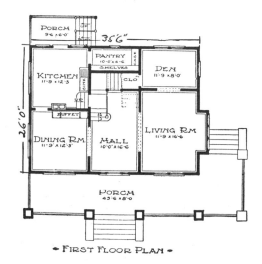

FIRST FLOOR PLAN

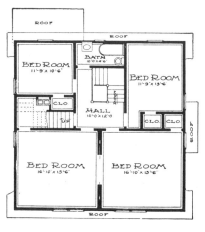

SECOND FLOOR PLAN

—12—

$1,446⁰⁰

For $1,446.00 we will furnish all the material to build this Nine-Room House, consisting of Lumber, Lath, Shingles, Mill Work, Ceiling, Flooring, Finishing Lumber, Buffet, Medicine Case, Building Paper, Pipe, Gutter, Sash Weights, Hardware and Painting Material. NO EXTRAS, as we guarantee enough material at the above price to build this house according to our plans.

By allowing a fair price for labor, cement, brick and plaster, which we do not furnish, this house can be built for about $2,730.00 including all material and labor.

For Our Offer of Free Plans See Page 3.

A COLONIAL two-story house with a gambrel roof. Large front porch, 45 feet 6 inches long by 8 feet wide, on the same level with which is an open porch or terrace, 12x10 feet. Large square porch columns, sided with shingles. Paneled lattice work under the porch, constructed with square porch balusters. Queen Anne windows. Reception hall, 10 feet wide by 16 feet 6 inches long, with large cased opening leading to the living room and cased opening leading to the dining room. Cased opening between the living room and den which can be used as a library. Oak open staircase to the landing, giving access to hall and kitchen. Large pantry. Two large bedrooms across the front on the second floor; double sliding doors between them. Two bedrooms in the rear; bathroom; and four closets.

Beauty oak veneered front door, 3x7 feet, 1¾ inches thick, glazed with bevel plate glass with side lights on each side, glazed with bevel plate glass. Two-panel veneered oak inside doors for the first floor; Craftsman design oak trim. Second floor, clear solid yellow pine five-cross panel doors and yellow pine trim. Clear oak flooring for the hall and main rooms on the first floor; clear maple flooring for the kitchen, pantry, entire second floor and porches of clear yellow pine. Plenty of large size windows make this house light and allow good ventilation.

Built on a concrete foundation, frame construction, sided and roofed with cedar shingles.

Painted two coats on all outside work except shingles, which are stained with creosote stain, color to suit owner. Varnish and wood filler for two coats of interior finish.

Excavated basement under the entire house, 7 feet from floor to joists, with cement floor. First floor, 9 feet from floor to ceiling; second floor, 8 feet 6 inches from floor to ceiling.

This house can be built on a lot 50 feet wide.

Complete Warm Air Heating Plant, for soft coal, extra	$103.51
Complete Warm Air Heating Plant, for hard coal, extra	105.72
Complete Hot Water Heating Plant, extra	256.94
Complete Steam Heating Plant, extra	218.10
Complete Plumbing Outfit, extra	120.29

SEARS, ROEBUCK AND CO.  **CHICAGO, ILLINOIS**

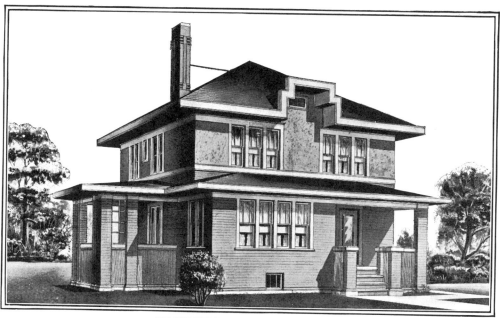

MODERN HOME No. 157

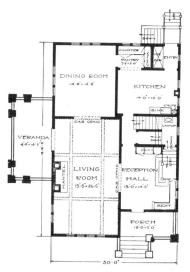

FIRST FLOOR

SECOND FLOOR

$1,717.00

For $1,717.00 we will furnish all the material to build this Eight-Room Residence, consisting of Mill Work, Ceiling, Siding, Flooring, Finishing Lumber, Building Paper, Pipe, Gutter, Sash Weights, Hardware, Mantel, Painting Material, Lumber, Lath and Shingles. NO EXTRAS, as we guarantee enough material at the above price to build this house according to our plans.

By allowing a fair price for labor, cement, brick and plaster, which we do not furnish, this house can be built for about $3,480.00, including all material and labor.

For Our Offer of Free Plans See Page 3.

A MODERN residence with exceptionally large living room 15 feet 6 inches by 26 feet 6 inches connected with the stair hall by means of a large cased opening and also connected with the dining room by a large cased opening. Every room is arranged to make the best use possible of all the available space. All the rooms on both first and second floors are large and well lighted and ventilated. The reception hall contains a Colonial combination wardrobe and closet with leaded art glass doors. Well proportioned open stairway. A long hall seat built in an L shape on two walls of the reception hall. The large living room on the first floor and the large chamber on the second floor each contains a mantel and fireplace.

Beauty doors for front and veranda entrances, veneered oak and glazed with bevel plate glass. The main rooms on the first floor are trimmed with clear oak casing, baseboard and molding; and six-cross panel oak doors; oak paneled beam ceiling in the living room. Second floor is trimmed with cypress casing, baseboard and molding and five-cross panel clear cypress doors. Clear oak flooring for reception hall, living room and dining room; maple flooring for kitchen and pantry; clear yellow pine flooring for the second floor and porches.

Front porch, 12x6 feet; large veranda, 9 feet 6 inches by 18 feet 6 inches, connected directly with the living room by a pair of double doors. This could very easily be screened in and used as an outdoor sleeping porch.

Built on a concrete foundation, frame construction, sided from the water table to window sills of the second story with narrow bevel edge cypress siding. The remainder of the house is finished with stonekote, more commonly known as cement plaster, and has cedar shingle roof on main house and porches.

Excavated basement under the entire house, 7 feet high from floor to joists. Rooms on the first floor are 9 feet from floor to ceiling; second floor, 8 feet 6 inches from floor to ceiling. Attic floored but not finished.

This house can be built on a lot 45 feet wide.

Complete Warm Air Heating Plant, for soft coal, extra	$132.57
Complete Warm Air Heating Plant, for hard coal, extra	135.03
Complete Hot Water Heating Plant, extra	288.20
Complete Steam Heating Plant, extra	225.75
Complete Plumbing Outfit, extra	156.31

SEARS, ROEBUCK AND CO.  **CHICAGO, ILLINOIS**

$2,533<u>00</u>

MODERN HOME No. 154

For $2,533.00 we will furnish all the material to build this Fourteen-Room Double House, consisting of Mill Work, Ceiling, Siding, Flooring, Finishing Lumber, Building Paper, Pipe, Gutter, Sash Weights, Medicine Cases, Buffets, Mantels, Hardware, Painting Material, Lumber, Lath and Shingles. NO EXTRAS, as we guarantee enough material at the above price to build this house according to our plans.

By allowing a fair price for labor, cement, brick and plaster, which we do not furnish, this house can be built for about $4,950.00, including all material and labor.

For Our Offer of Free Plans See Page 3.

A DOUBLE house built for two families. Has three rooms, stair hall and pantry on the first floor and three bedrooms, sewing room and bathroom on the second floor for each family. In this house we offer a very handy arrangement with a stair hall leading direct to the kitchen, dining room and parlor without having to pass through any of the other rooms. Inside cellar stairs directly under the main stairs. Large roomy closet off the center hall. On the second floor is a sewing room which is often used for a library; three good size bedrooms, a closet for each bedroom and a closet in each hall. Both bathrooms are close to each other so that the same pipes can be used for both, thereby making it possible to put in the plumbing at the very lowest possible cost. Each dining room contains a mantel, fireplace and buffet, with French bevel plate mirror.

Two Beauty front doors, veneered oak, glazed with bevel plate glass; leaded colored art glass transom overhead. The latest design of Queen Anne windows for front and sides. The six main rooms and halls are trimmed with oak Craftsman design of casing, baseboard and molding and two-panel veneered oak doors. Kitchen, pantry and entire second floor are trimmed with clear birch casing, baseboard and molding and two-panel veneered birch doors. Each front hall has an open oak staircase. Clear oak flooring for the front rooms and hall; maple flooring for kitchens and pantries; clear yellow pine flooring for the entire second floor and porches.

Hardware, lemon color brass finish.

This house presents the appearance of a large single residence and has practically no appearance of a double house from the exterior. Has a large front porch, 39 feet long by 9 feet wide, with Ionic columns put up in groups.

Built on a concrete block foundation, frame construction, sided with narrow bevel edge cypress siding from the water table to the second story window sills, and with stonekote, more commonly known as cement plaster, the rest of the way up. Gables sided with cedar shingles. Has a cedar shingle roof.

Painted two coats outside; your choice of color. Varnish and wood filler for two coats of interior finish.

Excavated basement under the entire building separated in two and making each basement private, 7 feet 6 inches from floor to joists, with cement floor. Rooms on the first floor are 9 feet 6 inches from floor to ceiling; second floor, 9 feet from floor to ceiling. A very large attic separated in two.

This house can be built on a lot 48 feet wide.

Complete Warm Air Heating Plant, for soft coal, extra	$181.78
Complete Warm Air Heating Plant, for hard coal, extra	184.04
Complete Steam Heating Plant, extra	329.38
Complete Hot Water Heating Plant, extra	360.95

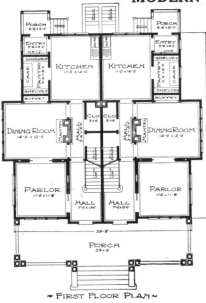

~FIRST FLOOR PLAN~

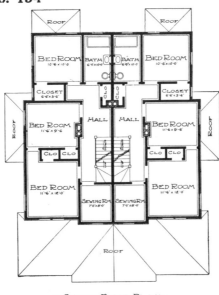

~SECOND FLOOR PLAN~

—14—

SEARS, ROEBUCK AND CO.  **CHICAGO, ILLINOIS**

MODERN HOME No. 129

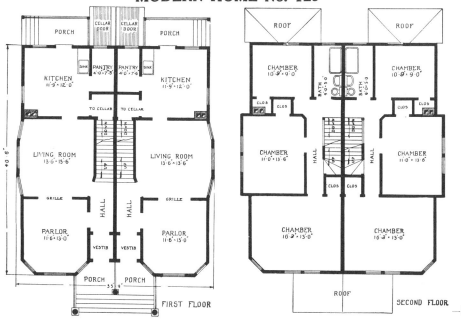

FIRST FLOOR

SECOND FLOOR

—15—

$1,632.00

For $1,632.00 we will furnish all the material to build this Twelve-Room Duplex House, consisting of Mill Work, Siding, Flooring, Ceiling, Finishing Lumber, Building Paper, Pipe, Gutter, Sash Weights, Hardware, Painting Material, Lumber, Lath and Shingles. NO EXTRAS, as we guarantee enough material at the above price to build this house according to our plans.

By allowing a fair price for labor, cement, brick and plaster, which we do not furnish, this house can be built for about $3,670.00, including all material and labor.

For Our Offer of Free Plans See Page 3.

A COZY double house for two families. Three rooms on the first floor and three rooms on the second floor for each family. Door leading from the stair hall to the parlor and another door leading from the stair hall to the living room, with grille between the parlor and living room. Large kitchen and pantry. Inside cellar stairway under the main stairs. Each room on the second floor opens directly into the stair hall. Large front bedroom; medium size rear bedroom and medium size middle bedroom. Each bedroom has a closet. Attic stairs directly over the main stairs.

Windsor front doors glazed with leaded glass. Blaine vestibule doors. Five-panel doors with yellow pine panels and soft pine stiles and rails. Clear yellow pine trim throughout the house. Yellow pine plate rail in the dining rooms. Yellow pine flooring for entire house and porches. Leaded Crystal windows for parlors and leaded Crystal attic sash.

Built on a concrete block foundation, frame construction, sided with narrow bevel edge cypress siding and has cedar shingle roof.

Painted two coats outside; your choice of color. Varnish and wood filler for interior finish.

Excavated basement under the entire house separated in two, making a private basement for each family. Basement, 7 feet 2 inches from floor to joists. First floor, 9 feet from floor to ceiling; second floor, 8 feet 6 inches from floor to ceiling. Large roomy attic separated in two, making a private attic for each family.

This house can be built on a lot 42 feet wide.

Complete Warm Air Heating Plant, for soft coal, extra	$170.32
Complete Warm Air Heating Plant, for hard coal, extra	175.00
Complete Steam Heating Plant, extra	277.85
Complete Hot Water Heating Plant, extra	292.85
Complete Plumbing Outfit, extra	208.00

SEARS, ROEBUCK AND CO.  **CHICAGO, ILLINOIS**

MODERN HOME No. 166

$1,095.00

For $1,095.00 we will furnish all the material to build this Seven-Room House, consisting of Mill Work, Flooring, Finishing Lumber, Building Paper, Pipe, Gutter, Sash Weights, Hardware, Painting Material, Lumber, Lath, Shingles and Porch Roofing. NO EXTRAS, as we guarantee enough material at the above price to build this house according to our plans.

By allowing a fair price for labor, cement, brick and plaster, which we do not furnish, this house can be built for about $2,706.00, including all material and labor.

For Our Offer of Free Plans See Page 3.

A COLONIAL stonekote house with brick veneered corners, veneered brick base and a large exterior brick chimney. Queen Anne windows and French front doors.

Hall doors are of Craftsman design, glazed with leaded art glass, with side lights glazed with leaded art glass to match. Large porch 8 feet wide by 42 feet long with brick columns.

A very handy arrangement of rooms. Open staircase to the second floor. Directly under the main stairs is a grade entrance from the outside which leads to either the kitchen or the basement.

On the first landing of the stairs are three windows, with a window seat 6 feet 6 inches long directly below the window sill. When you reach the second landing of the stairs you are within a very few feet of the entrance to all the rooms on the second floor. Closet for each bedroom and linen closet in the bathroom.

In the living room is a massive rustic fireplace. Sash on the right side of the dining room glazed with colored leaded art glass.

Latest design Craftsman oak doors on the first floor and oak open staircase. Clear birch doors and trim of Craftsman design on the second floor. Clear oak flooring for the living room, hall and dining room, and clear yellow pine flooring for the kitchen, pantry, entire second floor and porch.

Varnish and wood filler for two coats of interior finish.

Built on a concrete foundation, frame construction. Sided with brick veneer and stonekote; cedar shingle roof on the main house; Slate Surfaced Roofing for the porch.

Excavated basement under the entire house, 7 feet high from floor to joists, with cement floor. Rooms on the first floor are 9 feet from floor to ceiling; second floor, 8 feet from floor to ceiling. A large unfinished attic with three windows in the rear gable.

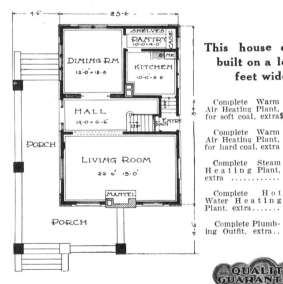

This house can be built on a lot 37 feet wide.

Complete Warm Air Heating Plant, for soft coal, extra	$ 84.57
Complete Warm Air Heating Plant, for hard coal, extra	87.01
Complete Steam Heating Plant, extra	196.73
Complete Hot Water Heating Plant, extra	240.22
Complete Plumbing Outfit, extra	115.52

QUALITY GUARANTEED

FIRST FLOOR PLAN

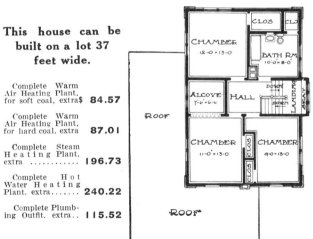

SECOND FLOOR PLAN

--16--

View of Living Room in Our Modern Home No. 166.

SEARS, ROEBUCK AND CO.   CHICAGO, ILL.

MODERN HOME No. 163

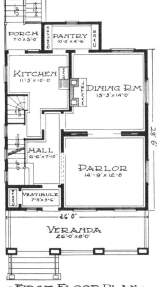

· FIRST FLOOR PLAN ·

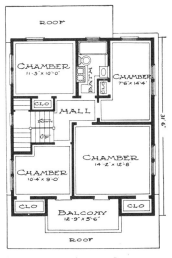

· SECOND FLOOR PLAN ·

$1,174.⁰⁰

For $1,174.00 we will furnish all the material to build this Eight-Room House, consisting of Mill Work, Flooring, Ceiling, Finishing Lumber, Building Paper, Pipe, Gutter, Sash Weights, Hardware, Mantel, Medicine Case, Lumber, Lath and Shingles. NO EXTRAS, as we guarantee enough material at the above price to build this house according to our plans.

By allowing a fair price for labor, cement, brick and plaster, which we do not furnish, this house can be built for about $2,675.00, including all material and labor.

For $64.00 extra we will furnish clear cypress bevel siding for the outside of this house.

For Our Offer of Free Plans See Page 3.

THIS house has two full stories and an attic. Sided with stonekote, more commonly known as cement plaster, which is fast becoming popular in many parts of the United States. It has a large front porch 26 feet long by 8 feet wide and a balcony over the porch 12 feet 9 inches long by 5 feet 6 inches wide. The main roof of the house extends over this balcony, which makes a very desirable place to be screened in and used as an open air sleeping porch.

Stair hall contains an open oak stairway to the second floor, under which is an inside cellar stairway; also a stairway from the kitchen leading to the second landing of the main stairs, enabling one to go to the second floor either from the front hall or from the kitchen. Outside cellar stairs under the rear porch. Cased opening between the hall and parlor. Sliding doors between parlor and dining room and a single door leading from the hall to the dining room, enabling one to go to the dining room from the hall without passing through the parlor; also a door to the kitchen from the hall. When on the second floor landing you are within a very few feet of the entrance to any of the four bedrooms or bathroom and to the attic stairs, thereby making good use of all the space possible. Colored leaded Art Nouveau sash at each stair landing and one about half way up the stairs; also in the vestibule near the front door. Mantel in the dining room.

Beauty front door, birch, 3x7 feet, 1¾ inches thick, glazed with bevel plate glass. Two-panel Wilcox veneered birch interior doors, with clear birch casing, baseboard and trim throughout the house. Two Dublin front doors on the second floor, one opening from each front chamber to the balcony. Clear oak flooring for the main rooms on the first floor; maple flooring for the kitchen, pantry and second floor; clear yellow pine edge grain flooring for the porches.

Varnish and wood filler for two coats of interior finish.

Built on a concrete foundation with concrete blocks above the grade line, frame construction, sided with stonekote and has cedar shingle roof.

Excavated basement under the entire house, 7 feet from floor to joists, with cement floor. Rooms on the first floor are 9 feet from floor to ceiling; second floor, 8 feet 6 inches from floor to ceiling, with a large roomy attic.

This house can be built on a lot 32 feet wide.

Complete Warm Air Heating Plant, for soft coal, extra	$ 90.43
Complete Warm Air Heating Plant, for hard coal, extra	94.05
Complete Hot Water Heating Plant, extra	206.47
Complete Steam Heating Plant, extra	174.29
Complete Plumbing Outfit, extra	117.50

SEARS, ROEBUCK AND CO.  **CHICAGO, ILLINOIS**

MODERN HOME No. 176

·FIRST·FLOOR·PLAN·

·SECOND·FLOOR·PLAN·

—18—

$2,006⁰⁰

For $2,006.00 we will furnish all the material to build this Eight-Room House, consisting of Lumber, Lath and Shingles, Mill Work, Flooring, Siding, Ceiling, Finishing Lumber, Building Paper, Pipe, Gutter, Sash Weights, Hardware, Brick Mantel, Buffet, Medicine Case, Painting Material, Bathroom Tile Floor. NO EXTRAS, as we guarantee enough material at the above price to build this house according to our plans.

By allowing a fair price for labor, cement, brick and plaster, which we do not furnish, this house can be built for about $3,800.00, including all material and labor.

For Our Offer of Free Plans See Page 3.

A LARGE modern type of square house with an open air dining porch and open air sleeping porch. The dining porch and sleeping porch may be enclosed with screen for the summer months and with sash during the winter months.

The top sash of the two-light windows, and also single windows are divided with wood bars. Priscilla sash frames in each dormer give this house a rich appearance and also afford a great deal of light in the attic, which is large enough for two small rooms. In the reception hall is an open oak stairway and large Colonial columns or colonnades reaching from the floor to the head casing, and in the living room is a Colonial fireplace. The dining room is separated from the living room by double sliding doors. The dining room has a Craftsman design oak buffet. Door leads from the dining room to the dining porch. The kitchen is exceptionally large, has a good size pantry with case on one side and shelving on the other and opens into the kitchen by means of a cased opening opposite the rear window, making it light and well ventilated. A closet between the pantry and the rear stairway is enclosed for a refrigerator and a storage for vegetables.

The stairs in the kitchen joins the landing of the main stairs, permitting one to go to the second floor from either the kitchen or reception hall. All bedrooms on the second floor have large closets and the two bedrooms on the left side of the house have mirror doors.

The flooring in the reception hall, living room and dining room is clear oak. The kitchen and pantries have clear maple flooring. The entire second story has yellow pine flooring, with the exception of the bathroom, which is of pure white tile. The first floor is of the latest Craftsman design, made of clear red oak, including doors and trim. The second floor has clear birch trim throughout. This house is built on a concrete block foundation and is of frame construction sided with clear cypress siding and has *A* cedar shingle roof.

Excavated basement under the entire house, 7 feet from the floor to joists. Rooms on the first floor have 9-foot ceilings. Rooms on the second floor have 9-foot ceilings.

This house can be built on a lot 38 feet wide.

Complete Warm Air Heating Plant, for soft coal, extra	$122.62
Complete Warm Air Heating Plant, for hard coal, extra	125.33
Complete Steam Heating Plant, extra	224.90
Complete Hot Water Heating Plant, extra	280.44
Complete Plumbing Outfit, extra	162.00

SEARS, ROEBUCK AND CO.  **CHICAGO, ILLINOIS**

MODERN HOME No. 178

$1,537⁰⁰

For $1,537.00 we will furnish all the material to build this Nine-Room House, consisting of Lumber, Lath, Shingles, Mill Work, Flooring, Siding, Ceiling, Finishing Lumber, Building Paper, Pipe, Gutter, Sash Weights, Hardware, Brick Mantel, Buffet, Medicine Case and Painting Material. NO EXTRAS, as we guarantee enough material at the above price to build this house according to our plans.

By allowing a fair price for labor, cement, brick and plaster, which we do not furnish, this house can be built for about $3,200.00, including all material and labor.

For Our Offer of Free Plans See Page 3.

A CRAFTSMAN style two-story house with a bungalow style roof. Top lights of windows are divided in square designs to harmonize with this style of architecture. The arches between the porch columns are raised high enough to give good light in the rooms on the second floor. The wide front porch extends across the entire front of house and is sided from the rail down to the grade line with wide boards. The house is sided with narrow beveled clear cypress siding.

The roof is shingled with *A* cedar shingles, and the porch flooring is made of edge grained fir 1⅛ inches thick.

The front door, also all interior doors and interior trim throughout, are clear red oak of latest Craftsman design. The large living room has an ornamental pressed brick fireplace with a bookcase at each side, and two seats, one at each end of bookcase, occupying the entire side of the living room. Two ceiling beams run crosswise of the living room, between which the fireplace is centered, also in the hall a ceiling is placed around the entire room.

For the dining room we also specify beamed ceiling and an oak buffet of latest Craftsman design. Open stairway made of clear red oak, clear oak flooring for the living room, reception hall and dining room. Maple flooring for the kitchen, pantry and entire second floor.

Built on a concrete block foundation. Has an excavated basement under the entire house, 7 feet high from floor to joists. Rooms on first floor, 9 feet to ceilings; on the second floor, 8 feet 6 inches to ceilings. Cement floor in basement.

We furnish paint for two coats on outside work, but a very desirable effect may be had by staining the siding with a brown stain and painting the finishing lumber and outside trim, door frames and window frames with pure white.

We also furnish sufficient filler and varnish to finish interior.

This house can be built on a lot 50 feet wide.

Complete Warm Air Heating Plant, for soft coal, extra	$103.19
Complete Warm Air Heating Plant, for hard coal, extra	105.88
Complete Steam Heating Plant, extra	226.15
Complete Hot Water Heating Plant, extra	300.79
Complete Plumbing Outfit, extra	168.00

SEARS, ROEBUCK AND CO.  **CHICAGO, ILLINOIS**

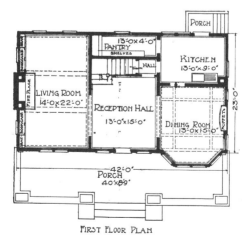

FIRST FLOOR PLAN

SECOND FLOOR PLAN

—19—

MODERN HOME No. 177

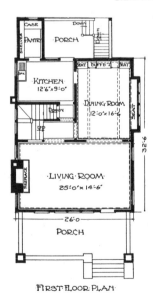

FIRST·FLOOR·PLAN·

SECOND·FLOOR·PLAN·

—20—

$1,414⁰⁰

For $1,414.00 we will furnish all the material to build this large Six-Room House, consisting of Lumber, Lath, Shingles, Mill Work, Flooring, Siding, Ceiling, Finishing Lumber, Building Paper, Pipe, Gutter, Sash Weights, Brick Mantel, Buffet, Medicine Case and Painting Material. NO EXTRAS, as we guarantee enough material at the above price to build this house according to our plans.

By allowing a fair price for labor, brick, cement and plaster, which we do not furnish, this house can be built for $3,100.00, including all material and labor.

For Our Offer of Free Plans See Page 3.

THIS combination of frame and cement plaster with wood panel strips, the latest style of construction has proven a great success. A wide front porch extends across the entire front. No columns in the center of the porch to obstruct the view.

The windows are of a design that are in harmony with the rest of the architectural scheme. The top sash of all two-light windows have divided wood bars, adding much to its appearance. In this house we specify the best clear narrow bevel cypress siding, the very best siding made. Roofs are covered with *A* cedar shingles. Porch floors are made of edge grain yellow pine flooring, ⅞ inch thick. Every room is perfectly lighted and well ventilated.

A glance at the floor plans will show that all rooms are very large and well located. The living room is 25 feet long by 14 feet 6 inches wide. The dining room is 16 feet 6 inches long by 12 feet wide. Bedrooms on the second floor are large size. A beautiful rustic fireplace with two colored art glass windows, one on each side, adorns this large and beautiful living room. Directly in the rear of the dining room is placed an oak buffet of the latest Craftsman design, and on each side of this buffet is placed seats. The buffet with the built-in seats covers the entire end of the room. The bay window in the dining room has four windows, making it a very well lighted room. Directly below these windows are built-in window seats. In addition to all this, this room has the latest style beam ceiling.

Beautiful double French design doors are placed between the living room and dining room, adding much to the beauty of both rooms. Cased openings lead from the living room to the stair hall, and cased openings from the stair hall to the dining room. Inside entry to the basement is conveniently placed directly under the main stairs. The latest Craftsman design clear red oak doors, stairwork and trim are furnished for the first floor. The doors and trim on the second floor are made of clear birch throughout. Clear oak flooring furnished for the living room, dining room and stair hall. Clear maple flooring furnished in kitchen, pantry and on the entire second floor. Bathroom floor is made of pure white tile. This house is built on a concrete foundation which extends 7 inches above the grade line and brick from that point to the wall sill.

Basement excavated 7 feet from the floor to joists. First floor rooms 9 feet to ceiling; second floor rooms, 8 feet 6 inches to ceiling.

We furnish paint for two coats for outside work and sufficient filler and varnish for interior work.

This house can be built on a lot 32 feet wide.

Complete Warm Air Heating Plant, for soft coal, extra	$ 96.13
Complete Warm Air Heating Plant, for hard coal, extra	98.82
Complete Steam Heating Plant, extra	185.05
Complete Hot Water Heating Plant, extra	233.11
Complete Plumbing Outfit, extra	168.00

SEARS, ROEBUCK AND CO.  **CHICAGO, ILLINOIS**

MODERN HOME No. 225

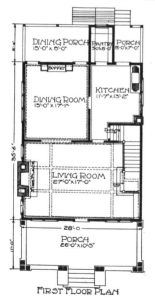

FIRST FLOOR PLAN

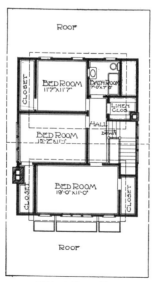

SECOND FLOOR PLAN

—21—

$1,381⁰⁰

For $1,381.00 we will furnish all the material to build this Seven-Room Bungalow, consisting of Lumber, Lath, Shingles, Mill Work, Flooring, Ceiling, Siding, Finishing Lumber, Building Paper, Pipe, Gutter, Sash Weights, Hardware and Painting Material. NO EXTRAS, as we guarantee enough material at the above price to build this house according to our plans.

By allowing a fair price for labor, cement, brick and plaster, which we do not furnish, this house can be built for about $2,800.00, including all material and labor.

For Our Offer of Free Plans See Page 3.

THIS charming bungalow will appeal to the discriminating home builder. The exterior is very attractive and has many good features. The long sloping roof relieved by the wide dormer, the grouping of columns at the corners of the porch, the flower boxes and the brick chimneys showing on the outside walls. The wide porch extending entirely across the front of the house, together with the open air dining room at the back of the house, afford plenty of room for outdoor living. The large living room is 17 feet wide by 27 feet long, has a beamed ceiling, a nicely planned stairway and a very attractive fireplace of molded brick. A large cased opening divides the living room from the dining room. A large Craftsman buffet of oak is built in across one end of the dining room. The kitchen has a good size pantry, in which is built a handy pantry case.

First Floor.

The front door is 1¾ inches thick, made of oak in the Craftsman style, glazed with rich plate glass. Inside doors are made in the Craftsman style, 1⅜ inches thick, of veneered oak, with Craftsman oak trim to match. Rear door is of white pine 1¾ inches thick, glazed with "A" quality double strength glass. Beamed ceiling in the living room, plate rail entirely around the dining room. Oak floor in the living room and dining room. Maple floor in the kitchen and pantry.

Second Floor.

An elegant oak stairway leads to the second floor. Doors are made of birch in the two-panel design, with birch trim to match. Good size clothes closet in each of the three bedrooms. Maple floor for the entire second floor, except in the bathroom, which has a mosaic tile floor.

Built on a concrete foundation. Framing timbers of the best No. 1 quality, and cedar shingles. Basement has cement floor and is 7 feet from floor to joists. First floor is 9 feet from floor to ceiling. Second floor, 7 feet 6 inches from floor to ceiling. Stain and paint for exterior, varnish and wood filler for interior.

This house requires a lot at least 50 feet wide to set it off properly.

Complete Warm Air Heating Plant, for soft coal, extra	$ 90.35
Complete Warm Air Heating Plant, for hard coal, extra	92.34
Complete Hot Water Heating Plant, extra	203.80
Complete Steam Heating Plant, extra	158.05
Complete Plumbing Outfit, extra	120.40

SEARS, ROEBUCK AND CO.  **CHICAGO, ILLINOIS**

MODERN HOME No. 172

$863.00

For $863.00 we will furnish all the material to build this Five-Room Bungalow, consisting of Lumber, Lath, Shingles, Mill Work, Flooring, Ceiling, Siding, China Closet, Finishing Lumber, Building Paper, Pipe, Gutter, Sash Weights, Hardware and Painting Material. **NO EXTRAS, as we guarantee enough material at the above price to build this house according to our plans.**

By allowing a fair price for labor, stone, concrete, brick and plaster, which we do not furnish, this bungalow can be built for about $1,600.00, including all material and labor.

For Our Offer of Free Plans See Page 3.

A MODERN bungalow of frame construction. Considered the best five-room bungalow ever built at anywhere near this low price. The extra wide siding, the visible rafters over porches and eaves give a pleasing rustic effect. The roof is ornamented by an attractive dormer with three windows. The front and side of the bungalow are beautified by many triple and double windows, making every room light and airy. The porch extends across the front of the house and is 29 feet 6 inches wide by 9 feet 6 inches deep, making a cool and shady retreat. Porch columns are arranged in clusters, supported by a base which is sided with the same material as used on the rest of the house.

First Floor.

The front entrance leads directly into a large parlor, size 15 feet by 13 feet 6 inches. Directly to the rear is located a large dining room, separated from the parlor by cased opening. Dining room is 18 feet long by 13 feet wide and has a sideboard or china closet and is trimmed with plate rail. Directly to the rear of this room is the kitchen, size 10 feet by 10 feet, with a door leading to the rear porch. The pantry being located between the kitchen and dining room makes it possible to use this room as a butler's serving pantry and pantry combined. On the left side of the house are located two large and airy chambers, size 13 feet by 13 feet 6 inches, with closets, and conveniently located between the two chambers is a bathroom, size 9 feet 6 inches by 9 feet 6 inches.

For the front door we furnish a heavy bevel plate glass door. Interior doors are five-cross panel yellow pine with clear yellow pine casings and trim throughout. Interior can be finished either light or dark finish, dark finish preferred. Clear yellow pine for the floor for the entire house and porches.

Built on concrete foundation, basement excavated and has cement floors. It is frame construction sided with 10-inch No. 1 boards and has a cedar shingle roof.

Height of Ceiling.

Basement, 7 feet from floor to joists.
First floor, 9 feet from floor to ceiling.
With small cost a very pleasing effect can be had by staining siding with brown creosote stain, and shingles with a moss green, all trimmings to be painted pure white. This same scheme has been followed with very satisfactory results.

This house can be built on a lot 40 feet wide.

Complete Warm Air Heating Plant, for soft coal, extra	$ 60.44
Complete Warm Air Heating Plant, for hard coal, extra	63.35
Complete Steam Heating Plant, extra	135.35
Complete Hot Water Heating Plant, extra	169.19
Complete Plumbing Outfit, extra	117.41

SEARS, ROEBUCK AND CO.  **CHICAGO, ILLINOIS**

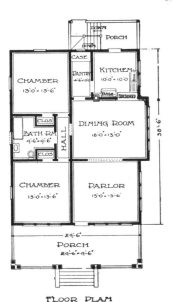

FLOOR PLAN

~ FIRST FLOOR PLAN ~

MODERN HOME No. 149

$1,742⁰⁰

For $1,742.00 we will furnish all the material to build this Eleven-Room Two-Family Flat Building, consisting of Mill Work, Ceiling, Siding, Flooring, Finishing Lumber, Hardware, Building Paper, Sash Weights, Medicine Cases, Buffets, Mantels, Painting Material, Lumber, Lath and Shingles. NO EXTRAS, as we guarantee enough material at the above price to build this house according to our plans.

~ SECOND FLOOR PLAN ~

By allowing a fair price for labor, cement, brick and plaster, which we do not furnish, this house can be built for about $3,520.00, including all material and labor.

For Our Offer of Free Plans See Page 3.

A MODERN two-family flat building in the Colonial style of architecture. Every inch of space is utilized to the best advantage.

Every room is very handy to the other rooms. Note the small amount of hall space compared with what is usually put into a building of this kind. A large vestibule with entrance to flat on the first floor and entrance to stairs for the second floor.

Each flat contains a mantel in the parlor, buffet in the dining room and medicine case in the bathroom. The library on the second floor contains bookcase built in the wall over the stairway leading from the first floor. The rear stairs are built inside of the house, enabling all the occupants of the building to go to the basement or to the attic without going outside.

Everything is up to date. Craftsman design veneered oak doors are specified. The vestibule, parlor and dining room on the first floor and the parlor, dining room and library on the second floor are trimmed with clear oak casing, base and moldings, with clear oak flooring. The remainder of both the first and second floors is trimmed with clear yellow pine casing, baseboard and molding, with five-cross yellow pine panel doors, clear maple flooring. The front stairs are clear oak and the rear stairs are clear yellow pine.

Note the large front porch, 22 feet long by 10 feet wide, with a balcony for the second floor of the same size, with a pair of double French doors leading from the library to this balcony. This affords the same amount of convenience and comfort for all occupants of the building. The columns on the front porch and balcony are of a heavy Colonial pattern, 10 inches in diameter. Porch floors are of clear yellow pine edge grain flooring.

The top sash of all the windows on the front and sides is divided into three lights and the bottom in one large light. This is a very late pattern and matches well with the Colonial style of building.

The rear entrance of the building is on the grade line, doing away with rear outside steps.

This house is built on a concrete foundation and is of frame construction. The main body is sided with bevel siding. The porch column bases and panels are covered with stonekote plaster. The balcony front and gables are sided with cedar shingles. Balance sided with narrow bevel edge cypress siding. Cedar shingles for the roof.

This house has an excavated basement under the entire house, 7 feet from floor to ceiling, with cement floor. Rooms on the first floor, 9 feet from floor to ceiling; rooms on second floor, 9 feet from floor to ceiling, with a very large attic, 8 feet from floor to collar beams, having ten sash, which makes a very convenient place for drying clothes and also a nice dry room for storage, etc.

Painted two coats outside; your choice of color. Varnish and wood filler for two coats of interior finish.

This house can be built on a lot 25 feet wide.

Complete Steam Heating Plant, extra...$209.48
Complete Hot Water Heating Plant, extra..255.99
Complete Plumbing Outfit, extra...229.19

SEARS, ROEBUCK AND CO.  **CHICAGO, ILLINOIS**

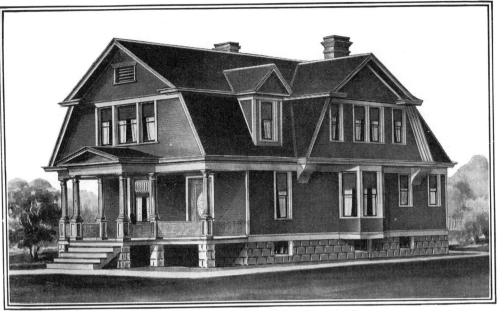

MODERN HOME No. 123

$1,328.00

For $1,328.00 we will furnish all the material to build this Nine-Room House, consisting of Lumber, Lath, Shingles, Mill Work, Flooring, Ceiling, Siding, Finishing Lumber, Building Paper, Pipe, Gutter, Sash Weights, Hardware and Painting Material. NO EXTRAS, as we guarantee enough material at the above price to build this house according to our plans.

By allowing a fair price for labor, cement, brick and plaster, which we do not furnish, this house can be built for about $2,835.00, including all material and labor.

For Our Offer of Free Plans See Page 3.

AN ATTRACTIVE two-story house of frame construction with gambrel roof, with return cornices. Arranged to give plenty of light and ventilation in every room in the house. Front porch, 27 feet long by 7 feet wide, is covered by the projection of the second story and supported by massive Colonial columns with square paneled base. The projection on porch is 10x5 feet and is in harmony with the general lines of the house.

Entrance on grade line on the left hand side leading to the kitchen and to the basement.

Front vestibule leads into large reception hall which has an attractive oak staircase leading to the second floor. To the right of the vestibule is a closet, also closet directly under stairs. Oak grille divides reception hall from living room. Living room has attractive quarter sawed oak mantel and tile fireplace and large fancy window. Large dining room, which is conveniently located, has a bay window, and is trimmed with plate rail. Between living room and kitchen is a good size bedroom which can be used as a library. The large kitchen has entrance to side and also to the rear, with stairs going to the basement and to second floor. Adjoining kitchen is a pantry with drawers and shelves, and entry leading to back steps.

First Floor.

Front door made of oak 1¾ inches thick, with bevel plate glass. Inside doors, with exception of kitchen and pantry, are six-cross panel oak with oak trim to match oak plate rail in dining room. Kitchen and pantry doors are five-cross panel white pine with trim to match. All floors, with the exception of kitchen, bedroom and pantry, are clear oak. Kitchen, bedroom and pantry floors are of clear maple, all laid on yellow pine floor lining.

Second Floor.

Stairs from first floor lead to hall on second floor. This hall leads to extra large bedroom in the front and three medium size bedrooms and bathroom. All bedrooms have closets, with shelf in each. All rooms are light and airy. All doors and trim are made of clear white pine; all floors are of clear yellow pine.

Built on concrete block foundation and excavated under entire house. We furnish clear cypress siding and cedar shingles. Framing timbers of best quality yellow pine. Leaded Crystal glass front window. All windows "A" quality double strength glass.

Basement, 7 feet 4 inches from floor to joist, with cement floor.
First floor, 8 feet 6 inches from floor to ceiling.
Second floor, 8 feet 6 inches from floor to ceiling.
Painted with two coats of best paint outside. Varnish and wood filler for interior finish.

This house can be built on a lot 31 feet 6 inches wide.

Complete Warm Air Heating Plant, for soft coal, extra $108.87
Complete Warm Air Heating Plant, for hard coal, extra 111.58
Complete Steam Heating Plant, extra 171.50
Complete Hot Water Heating Plant, extra 207.87
Complete Plumbing Outfit, extra 139.09

SEARS, ROEBUCK AND CO.  CHICAGO, ILLINOIS

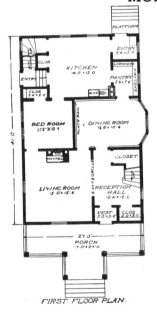

FIRST FLOOR PLAN.

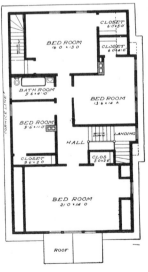

SECOND FLOOR PLAN

MODERN HOME No. 148

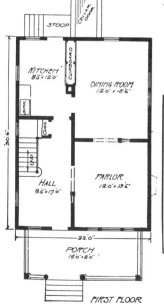

FIRST FLOOR

SECOND FLOOR

—25—

$932⁰⁰

For $932.00 we will furnish all the material to build this Eight-Room House, consisting of Mill Work, Flooring, Ceiling, Siding, Finishing Lumber, Building Paper, Eaves Trough, Hardware, Painting Material, Lumber, Lath and Shingles. NO EXTRAS, as we guarantee enough material at the above price to build this house according to our plans.

By allowing a fair price for labor, cement, brick and plaster, which we do not furnish, this house can be built for about $1,980.00, including all material and labor.

For Our Offer of Free Plans See Page 3.

IN MODERN Home No. 148 we have a good substantial house of nice appearance, suitable for suburban residence or country home. As will be seen from the floor plan shown below, every bit of space in this house has been used to the best advantage, leaving absolutely no waste space. The exterior leaves nothing to be desired in appearance. There are four windows in each front bedroom on the second floor which admit an abundance of air and light and will be found even more practical than an outdoor sleeping room. A large porch, 8 feet by 19 feet, extends entirely across the front of the house.

As one enters the hall, the first thing to be seen is a nice open oak staircase with a landing half way up to the second floor. Three nice rooms on the first floor, all of which, excepting the kitchen, are finished in oak; the kitchen being finished in yellow pine, with maple flooring. The interior doors on the first floor are two-panel oak veneered.

The feature of this house is the combination china closet and cupboard placed between the dining room and kitchen, opening into both rooms. This arrangement makes all parts of the cupboard accessible from either the kitchen or dining room, saving many steps. On the second floor are four nice bedrooms and bath, with a fair size closet in each bedroom. The second floor is finished in clear yellow pine with five-cross panel doors, having yellow pine panels with clear soft pine stiles and rails. Clear yellow pine flooring is furnished for the second floor and porch.

This house is of frame construction, built on concrete block foundation. Is sided up to the second story window sills with narrow bevel edge cypress siding, and cedar shingles up the rest of the way to the cornice. It also has cedar shingle roof. Painted two coats outside; color to suit. Varnish and wood filler for two coats of interior finish.

Excavated basement under the entire house, 7 feet from floor to joist with cement floor. First floor, 9 feet from floor to ceiling; second floor, 8 feet from floor to ceiling.

This house can be built on a lot 28 feet wide.

Complete Warm Air Heating Plant, for soft coal, extra	$ 82.25
Complete Warm Air Heating Plant, for hard coal, extra	85.16
Complete Steam Heating Plant, extra	172.73
Complete Hot Water Heating Plant, extra	208.68
Complete Plumbing Outfit, extra	113.70

SEARS, ROEBUCK AND CO.  **CHICAGO, ILLINOIS**

MODERN HOME No. 228

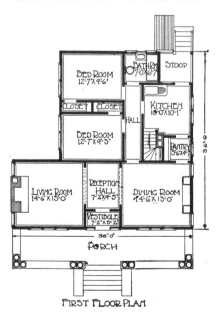

FIRST FLOOR PLAN

—26—

$1,182.00

For $1,182.00 we will furnish all the material to build this Six-Room Bungalow, consisting of Lumber, Lath, Shingles, Mill Work, Flooring, Ceiling, Siding, China Closet, Fireplace, Finishing Lumber, Building Paper, Pipe, Gutter, Sash Weights, Hardware and Painting Material. NO EXTRAS, as we guarantee enough material at the above price to build this house according to our plans.

By allowing a fair price for labor, stone, concrete and plaster, which we do not furnish, this bungalow can be built for about $2,200.00, including all material and labor.

For Our Offer of Free Plans See Page 3.

A WELL designed bungalow is the most attractive of all styles of houses. With this in mind, our architect has designed what may truly be termed a perfect bungalow. One is impressed with the exterior appearance, the wide projecting eaves, the low lines suggesting room and comfort.

On entering this house one passes through the vestibule into the reception hall, which has a large cased opening on both sides, making practically one large room out of the reception hall, living room and dining room. The living room has a massive brick fireplace, on either side of which is a large colored art glass window. The dining room has a large Craftsman oak buffet built in, with a leaded art glass sash on each side. The kitchen is just a convenient size, being 10 feet by 10 feet 1 inch. The entrance to the dining room from the kitchen is through the pantry. There are two nice bedrooms, each having a good size clothes closet.

First Floor.

The front and vestibule doors are 1¾ inches thick, made of oak in the Craftsman style, each door having eight small lights of bevel plate glass. All interior doors are of the Craftsman style with Craftsman trim in oak to match. The rear door is of soft pine, 1¾ inches thick, glazed with plain "A" quality double strength glass. Oak floors in every room, with the exception of the kitchen and bathroom, these two rooms have maple flooring.

Basement.

Basement under entire house, 7 feet from floor to joists; cement floor. Both outside and inside stairways.

Built on a concrete foundation. Excavated under entire house. This house is roofed with cedar shingles and all framing timbers are of the best quality. Windows are of Colonial pattern and glazed with "A" quality glass. First floor is 9 feet from floor to ceiling. Basement 7 feet from floor to joists.

Stain and paint furnished for the outside, varnish and wood filler for interior finish.

This bungalow can be built on a lot 40 feet wide.

Complete Warm Air Heating Plant, for soft coal, extra.........................$ 57.46
Complete Warm Air Heating Plant, for hard coal, extra............................ 60.74
Complete Hot Water Heating Plant, extra....................................... 160.35
Complete Steam Heating Plant, extra... 124.85
Complete Plumbing Outfit, extra... 118.54

MODERN HOME No. 174

FIRST FLOOR

SECOND FLOOR

$889⁰⁰

For $889.00 we will furnish all the material to build this Five-Room House with attic, consisting of Mill Work, Flooring, Ceiling, Siding, Finishing Lumber, Buffet, Medicine Case, Pantry Case, Building Paper, Pipe, Gutter, Sash Weights, Hardware, Mantel, Painting Material, Lumber, Lath and Shingles. NO EXTRAS, as we guarantee enough material at the above price to build this house according to our plans.

By allowing a fair price for labor, concrete blocks, brick and plaster, which we do not furnish, this house can be built for about $1,800.00, including all material and labor.

For Our Offer of Free Plans See Page 3.

MODERN Home No. 174 was designed particularly for a narrow lot. It is possible to build this house on a lot 22 feet wide. A large porch 18 feet long by 7 feet deep extends across the entire front of the house. Nearly all the windows are of Colonial pattern. Front door is our Dublin pattern oak, glazed with bevel plate glass. As will be seen by the picture, the glass extends from the top of the door down to within 18 inches of the bottom. All the inside doors are of clear yellow pine. Open stairway leading from the hall to the second floor. The casing, base, window stool; in fact, all the inside trim and flooring is of clear yellow pine. The doors are of the five-cross panel style. Double sliding doors separate the dining room from the parlor. We particularly call your attention to the many nice features in the large dining room. Brick mantel and fireplace in the corner. A beautiful buffet is built in, with plate rail around the entire room. The window seat extends entirely across the bay. The kitchen is a small room 10 feet 6 inches by 10 feet, having a fair size pantry and closet.

On the second floor are two good size bedrooms, each having a clothes closet. The bathroom is at the end of the hall. The front bedroom on the second floor has an alcove 6 feet by 6 feet 3 inches in one corner with window seats.

Painted two coats outside; your choice of color. Varnish and wood filler for interior finish.

Built on a concrete block foundation, frame construction, sided with narrow bevel edge cypress siding. Cedar shingles for roof and porches.

Rooms on first floor, 9 feet from floor to ceiling; second floor, 8 feet from floor to ceiling.

Excavated basement under the entire house with cement floor. 7 feet from cement floor to rafters.

This house can be built on a lot 22 feet wide.

Complete Warm Air Heating Plant, for soft coal, extra.$	**67.10**
Complete Warm Air Heating Plant, for hard coal, extra	**69.58**
Complete Steam Heating Plant, extra..................	**148.35**
Complete Hot Water Heating Plant, extra.............	**188.07**
Complete Plumbing Outfit, extra......................	**125.34**

SEARS, ROEBUCK AND CO.  **CHICAGO, ILLINOIS**

MODERN HOME No. 191

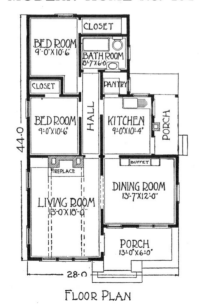

FLOOR PLAN

$885.00

For $885.00 we will furnish all the material to build this Five-Room Bungalow consisting of Lumber, Lath, Shingles, Mill Work, Flooring, Ceiling, Finishing Lumber, Building Paper, Pipe, Gutter, Sash Weights, Hardware and Painting Material. NO EXTRAS, as we guarantee enough material at the above price to build this house according to our plans.

By allowing a fair price for labor, cement, brick and plaster, which we do not furnish, this house can be built for about $1,800.00, including all material and labor.

For Our Offer of Free Plans See Page 3.

THIS California Bungalow has many points to recommend to the home builder who desires a real home, a dwelling that is something more than a place to exist.

The exterior leaves nothing to be desired. Sided with rough boards up to the height of 9 feet from the ground and stonekote or stucco under the wide overhanging eaves. There are two entrances to this bungalow from the front porch, one being a French door which opens into the dining room, the other a Craftsman door which opens into the living room. The living room with its beamed ceiling, rustic brick fireplace and built-in seat alongside of the fireplace, is a large airy apartment, having three large windows and two sash which admit an abundance of light and air. The dining room is also a good size room and has an attractive buffet of oak built in one side. There are two bedrooms and a bathroom, each of the two bedrooms having a good size clothes closet. The kitchen is just the right size, has a nice pantry in which is built a pantry case.

This house can be finished with siding instead of stonekote at about the same price for the complete house.

Front door is of oak, 1¾ inches thick and made in the Craftsman style. Dining room door is made of oak, 1¾ inches thick and is the French style of door, having small sash extending from bottom of the door entirely to the top. All inside doors are oak, made in the Craftsman style. The rear door is 1¾ inches thick, made of soft pine and glazed with the best quality double strength glass. Craftsman oak trim throughout the house. Oak floor in the living and dining rooms, and maple floor in the bedrooms and kitchen. Mosaic tile floor is furnished for the bathroom.

Built on a concrete foundation. Excavated under the entire house. We furnish cedar shingles and the best No. 1 quality framing timbers and siding.

Basement has a cement floor and is 7 feet from floor to joists. First floor is 9 feet from floor to ceiling.

Stain and paint for outside, varnish and wood filler for the interior finish.

This house, while it is only 28 feet wide, requires a lot at least 40 feet wide to set it off properly.

Complete Warm Air Heating Plant, for soft coal, extra	$ 56.44
Complete Warm Air Heating Plant, for hard coal, extra	59.72
Complete Steam Heating Plant, extra	126.70
Complete Hot Water Heating Plant, extra	155.81
Complete Plumbing Outfit, extra	119.00

SEARS, ROEBUCK AND CO.  **CHICAGO, ILLINOIS**

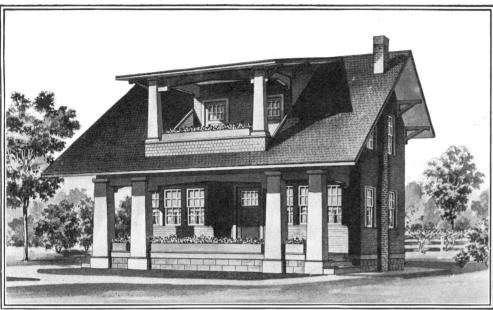

MODERN HOME No. 162.　Yellow Pine Finish.
MODERN HOME No. 162½.　Oak Finish.

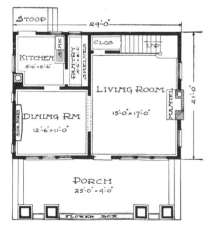

FIRST FLOOR

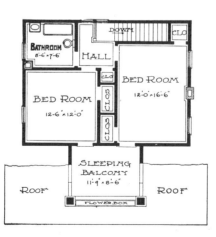

SECOND FLOOR

$832⁰⁰

For $832.00 we will furnish all the material to build this Five-Room Bungalow, consisting of Mill Work, Flooring, Ceiling, Siding, Finishing Lumber, China Closet, Building Paper, Pipe, Gutter, Sash Weights, Hardware, Mantel, Painting Material, Lumber, Lath and Shingles and Best-of-all Felt Roofing for roof over Sleeping Balcony. NO EXTRAS, as we guarantee enough material at the above price to build this house according to our plans.

By allowing a fair price for labor, cement, brick and plaster, which we do not furnish, this house can be built for about $1,630.00, including all material and labor.

For Our Offer of Free Plans See Page 3.

A FIVE-ROOM bungalow of Craftsman style with front porch 25 feet long by 9 feet wide, and open air sleeping balcony 11 feet 9 inches by 8 feet 6 inches.
Front door opens into a large living room 17x15 feet, which has a quarter sawed oak mantel, staircase, closed under stairs. Living room has three front windows, also one window on each side of fireplace. Cased opening leads from living room to dining room. Dining room has sideboard facing the cased opening with leaded glass sash on each side, also three windows in the front. Also plate rail around the entire room.
Double swinging door leads to kitchen, which has one window directly over the sink, another on the side. Pantry is convenient to kitchen or dining room.
For No. 162, first and second floor trimmed in yellow pine, we furnish front door 3x7 feet, 1¾ inches thick, with a long bevel plate glass. Inside doors are five-cross panel yellow pine. Clear yellow pine trim and flooring.

First Floor.

For No. 162½ we furnish front doors, also inside doors and moldings of clear red oak in the latest Craftsman design. Clear red oak flooring for the living room and dining room. Maple flooring for kitchen and pantry.

Second Floor.

Trimmed in oak. We furnish front door leading to the balcony and inside doors and trim of clear red oak, Craftsman design, and clear maple flooring.
Stairs on second floor are within arm's reach of either bedrooms or bathroom. One bedroom, 12 feet by 16 feet 6 inches, has two closets and door leading to sleeping balcony, also two windows on the side. Other bedroom, 12 feet 6 inches by 12 feet, has one closet and door leading to sleeping balcony, and window on the side.
Bathroom is 7 feet 6 inches by 8 feet 6 inches. Walls up to height of 4 feet 6 inches finished in cement and cut to imitate tile and white enamel. A linen closet in hall.

Built on a concrete block foundation, excavated basement under entire building. Frame construction and sided with clear red wood bevel siding. Shingled with *A* shingles. All framing lumber is No. 1 yellow pine.
Paint furnished for two coats of outside, your choice of color. Varnish and wood filler for two coats, interior hard oil finish.
Basement has cement floor. Basement, 7 feet high from floor to joists.
First floor, 9 feet from floor to ceiling.
Second floor, 8 feet 6 inches from floor to ceiling.
We furnish our No. 162½, which is the same as No. 162, with the exception that it is trimmed with clear Craftsman oak doors and moldings throughout and hardwood flooring as specified above, for $146.00 extra. If you want this house trimmed in oak send for plan No. 162½.

This house can be built on a lot 35 feet wide.

Complete Warm Air Heating Plant, for soft coal, extra	$ 74.94
Complete Warm Air Heating Plant, for hard coal, extra	78.50
Complete Steam Heating Plant, extra	143.97
Complete Hot Water Heating Plant, extra	187.11
Complete Plumbing Outfit, extra	105.75

SEARS, ROEBUCK AND CO.  **CHICAGO, ILLINOIS**

$939⁰⁰

For $939.00 we will furnish all the material to build this Six-Room House, consisting of Lumber, Lath, Shingles, Mill Work, Flooring, Ceiling, Siding, Finishing Lumber, Building Paper, Pipe, Gutter, Sash Weights, Hardware and Painting Material. **NO EXTRAS**, as we guarantee enough material at the above price to build this house according to our plans.

By allowing a fair price for labor, cement, brick and plaster, which we do not furnish, this house can be built for about $1,850.00, including all material and labor.

For Our Offer of Free Plans See Page 3.

WHILE this house can be built for a very reasonable amount, it has the appearance of a $3,000.00 house, arranged to give an abundance of light and ventilation in every room. Front porch is 24 feet wide by 7 feet 6 inches deep, and on account of its being sided up to the porch rail it could be screened in at very little expense. The front door opens into the reception hall, which has an attractive staircase leading to the second floor. The cased opening between the living room and reception hall practically makes one large room of these two rooms. The living room, which is also used as a dining room, is 12 feet wide by 15 feet 2 inches long. The kitchen is 13 feet 4 inches by 10 feet 6 inches and has a good size pantry. The bathroom is on the first floor.

First Floor.

Front door is made of soft pine, 1¾ inches thick, glazed with bevel plate glass. Inside doors are of the five-cross panel style and made of the best quality yellow pine, the same grade of yellow pine being used for inside trim and floors.

Second Floor.

The stairway from the first floor leads to a hall on the second floor from which any one of the three bedrooms and linen closet can be reached. These three bedrooms have splendid ventilation, there being windows on two sides of each room. Doors are five-cross panel and made of the best quality yellow pine, with trim and flooring to match.

Built on a brick foundation and excavated basement under entire house. We furnish clear cypress siding and cedar shingles, framing timbers of the best quality yellow pine. All windows "A" quality glass. Basement has cement floor.

Height of Ceilings.

Basement, 7 feet from floor to joists.
First floor, 9 feet from floor to ceiling.
Second floor, 8 feet from floor to ceiling.
Painted two coats of best paint outside, varnish and wood filler for interior finish.

This house can be built on a lot 35 feet wide.

Complete Warm Air Heating Plant, for soft coal, extra	$ 70.77
Complete Warm Air Heating Plant, for hard coal, extra	75.01
Complete Steam Heating Plant, extra	138.95
Complete Hot Water Heating Plant, extra	171.35
Complete Plumbing Outfit, extra	119.73

MODERN HOME No. 179

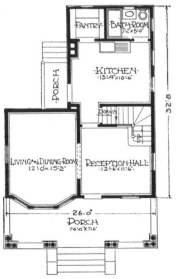

-FIRST-FLOOR-PLAN-

-SECOND-FLOOR-PLAN-

—30—

SEARS, ROEBUCK AND CO.  **CHICAGO, ILLINOIS**

MODERN HOME No. 124

$1,103.00

For $1,103.00 we will furnish all the material to build this Nine-Room Two-Story Bungalow, consisting of Mill Work, Ceiling, Siding, Flooring, Finishing Lumber, Building Paper, Pipe, Gutter, Sash Weights, Hardware, Painting Material, Mantel, Lumber, Lath and Shingles. NO EXTRAS, as we guarantee enough material at the above price to build this bungalow according to our plans.

By allowing a fair price for labor, cement, brick and plaster, which we do not furnish, this house can be built for about $2,156.00 including all material and labor.

For Our Offer of Free Plans See Page 3.

A BUNGALOW which is fast becoming a great favorite in the Central, Eastern and Western states. This bungalow is so arranged that the large reception hall, dining room and extra large living room practically open into one. A very unique arrangement of open staircase in the rear of the reception hall leading to the second floor. A mantel in the center of the living room. All these rooms have a perfect view to the front porch and street. Every room is perfectly lighted and ventilated. The hall on the second floor has a splendid light coming over the open staircase from the four second story windows in the rear, making the reception hall on the first floor a well lighted room.

We furnish our Victoria front door, glazed leaded glass, and clear solid five-cross panel yellow pine doors for both first and second floors. With clear yellow pine trim, such as casing, baseboard, molding, etc. Clear yellow pine flooring for entire house and porch. Windows divided into eight and twelve lights, which are in perfect harmony with the bungalow architecture. Can be finished with Craftsman hardwood trim at a small advance in price.

Large front porch, 9 feet wide by 42 feet long. The rear door is on the grade line, thereby doing away with any steps in the rear.

Painted two coats outside; your choice of color. Wood filler and varnish for two coats of interior finish.

There is an excavated cellar, 10x14 feet, 7 feet from floor to joists. The rooms on the first floor are 9 feet from floor to ceiling; second floor, 8 feet from floor to ceiling. This bungalow is built on a concrete block foundation, frame construction, sided with narrow bevel edge cypress siding and has cedar shingle roof.

This bungalow can be built on a lot 48 feet wide.

Complete Warm Air Heating Plant, for soft coal, extra	$ 90.49
Complete Warm Air Heating Plant, for hard coal, extra	93.50
Complete Steam Heating Plant, extra	220.25
Complete Hot Water Heating Plant, extra	280.54
Complete Plumbing Outfit, extra	115.00

SEARS, ROEBUCK AND CO.  **CHICAGO, ILLINOIS**

FIRST FLOOR.   SECOND FLOOR.

MODERN HOME No. 151

$1,235⁰⁰

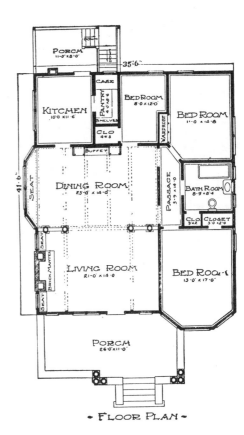

- FLOOR PLAN -

For $1,235.00 we will furnish all the material to build this Six-Room Bungalow, consisting of Mill Work, Ceiling, Siding, Flooring, Finishing Lumber, Building Paper, Pipe, Gutter, Sash Weights, Buffet, Medicine Case, Pantry Case, Hardware, Painting Material, Lumber, Lath and Shingles. NO EXTRAS, as we guarantee enough material at the above price to build this house according to our plans.

By allowing a fair price for labor, cement, brick and plaster, which we do not furnish, this house can be built for about $2,885.00, including all material and labor.

For Our Offer of Free Plans See Page 3.

A FINE example of a modern bungalow, conveniently arranged, perfectly lighted and ventilated with a great many large windows. Very large living room and dining room connected with arch opening, and four massive Colonial columns and balustrades. Paneled beam ceiling in each of these two rooms. Rustic brick fireplace in the living room with seat built on each side, and colored leaded art glass sash over each seat.

To appreciate the nice features of this bungalow see page 33, where we show an illustration of the interior of part of the living room and dining room, showing the Craftsman buffet, window seats, Colonial columns and balustrades, arches, colored leaded art glass, beam ceilings, etc.

Note the large front bedroom with bay window, and closet provided for each bedroom, also the linen closet for the bathroom. Doors, inside molding and trim are all oak and of the latest Craftsman design. Oak flooring for all rooms excepting the kitchen, back bedroom, bathroom and pantry, which have maple flooring. Clear yellow pine flooring for porches.

Painted two coats outside; your choice of color. Varnish and wood filler for interior finish.

Built on a concrete block foundation. Excavated basement under the entire house, 7 feet high to the joists, with cement floor. Rooms on the main floor are 9 feet 4 inches from floor to ceiling. Sided with narrow beveled edge siding of clear cypress and shingled with **cedar shingles.**

This bungalow can be built on a lot 40 feet wide.

Complete Warm Air Heating Plant, for soft coal, extra	$ 77.72
Complete Warm Air Heating Plant, for hard coal, extra	80.47
Complete Steam Heating Plant, extra	155.10
Complete Hot Water Heating Plant, extra	198.90
Complete Plumbing Outfit, extra	118.04

SEARS, ROEBUCK AND CO.  **CHICAGO, ILLINOIS**

Living and Dining Room of Our Bungalow No. 151

This illustration is an exact reproduction of the interior of our Bungalow No. 151, looking through the living room into the dining room, and is a perfect picture of simple elegance and homelike comfort.

Note the large rustic brick fireplace with a leaded art glass sash and a seat on each side. The Colonial columns and balustrade work are new and up to date features which are being used only in high priced houses. From the first impression you would think this house would cost over $4,000.00, but we make it possible for you to build it for less than $2,900.00.

Compare this house with similar houses already built in your neighborhood at a cost of from $4,000.00 to $5,000.00. There are many reasons why such homes are usually very expensive. Architects charge all the way from $100.00 to $150.00 for a set of plans and specifications. This is the amount we save you to start with, and our competent, practical and expert architects specify stock sizes and patterns of doors, windows, trim, etc.,

which enables you to buy your materials for several hundred dollars less than you could buy them if they were furnished according to ordinary architects' specifications, which in most cases are odd sizes and patterns and have to be made to order.

We own our own saw mill and ship lumber direct from our mill to you. We also control the output of one of the biggest mill work factories in the country and ship all doors, windows, moldings, in fact, a complete line of mill work and building materials, direct to you. In this way we save you several hundred dollars which is usually paid for profits to jobbers and retail dealers.

Don't build until you have had our quotations on materials.

Our plans are so complete in every detail that any ordinary workman can build any one of the houses shown in this book, with no lost time whatever to figure out how the different parts are to be put together.

MODERN HOME No. 168

FLOOR PLAN

SAVED $700.00 ON ONE ORDER.

Cheyenne, Wyo.

Sears, Roebuck and Co., Chicago, Ill.

Gentlemen:—In regard to carload of mill work and finishing lumber would say that by purchasing same from your firm I was enabled to save at least $700.00 on an eight-room house. When one considers that quarter sawed oak flooring may be purchased from you at $48.00 per 1,000 feet as against $100.00 per 1,000 feet in this locality, the saving on 1,000 feet of quarter sawed oak flooring alone was sufficient to pay one-half the freight charges on the entire carload. As to the quality of the lumber and mill work would say that the goods speak for themselves as being A 1. The promptness of delivery when nothing but stock sizes are ordered appeals to me so strongly that I am now daily expecting the arrival of a carload of mill work ordered from you about ten days ago. Assuring you of my continued patronage, I remain.

Yours truly,
L. P. DESMOND, M. D

$1,085.00

For $1,085.00 we will furnish all the material to build this Five-Room Bungalow, consisting of Mill Work, Ceiling, Flooring, Finishing Lumber, Building Paper, Pipe, Gutter, Sash Weights, Buffet, Medicine Case, Pantry Case, Hardware, Painting Material, Lumber, Lath and Shingles. NO EXTRAS, as we guarantee enough material at the above price to build this house according to our plans.

By allowing a fair price for labor, cement, brick and plaster, which we do not furnish, this house can be built for about $2,075.00, including all material and labor.

For Our Offer of Free Plans See Page 3.

A MODERN type of bungalow, sided with cedar shingles and having exterior brick chimney. Large front porch, 16 feet 6 inches by 7 feet. Large dining room which contains Craftsman buffet and mantel. Colored leaded art glass sash on each side of the mantel. Large living room with nook and seat; three colored leaded art sash. Pantry opens to the dining room and the kitchen. Open closet off the hall with sash between this closet and the pantry for light. Inside stairs to the basement, also outside cellar stairs under the rear porch.

Craftsman front door, glazed with leaded art glass. All interior doors and trim of oak and of the latest Craftsman design. Clear red oak flooring for living room and dining room, clear maple flooring for bedrooms, kitchen and bathroom, and clear yellow pine flooring for porches.

Built on a concrete foundation and is of frame construction, sided and roofed with cedar shingles; front gable is sided with stonekote, more commonly known as cement plaster.

The attic can be finished up to very good advantage at a small cost, and the stairway could be placed directly over the cellar stairs, thereby doing away with the open closet which is now shown on the plan.

Painted two coats outside; your choice of color. Varnish and wood filler for interior finish.

Excavated basement under the entire house, 7 feet from floor to joists, with cement floor. Rooms on main floor are 9 feet from floor to ceiling.

This house can be built on a lot 34 feet wide.

Complete Warm Air Heating Plant, for soft coal, extra	$ 59.71
Complete Warm Air Heating Plant, for hard coal, extra	62.97
Complete Steam Heating Plant, extra	127.95
Complete Hot Water Heating Plant, extra	161.76
Complete Plumbing Outfit, extra	114.70

SEARS, ROEBUCK AND CO.  **CHICAGO, ILLINOIS**

MODERN HOME No. 126

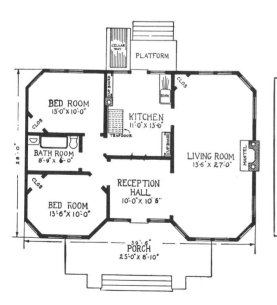

$776.00

For $776.00 we will furnish all the material to build this Six-Room Bungalow, consisting of Mill Work, Flooring, Ceiling, Finishing Lumber, Building Paper, Pipe, Gutter, Sash Weights, Mantel, Hardware, Painting Material, Lumber, Lath and Shingles. **NO EXTRAS,** as we guarantee enough material at the above price to build this house according to our plans.

By allowing a fair price for labor, cement, brick and plaster, which we do not furnish, this house can be built for about $1,615.00, including all material and labor.

For Our Offer of Free Plans See Page 3.

EVERY room in the house is well lighted and ventilated. Both bedrooms adjoin the bathroom. A large reception hall opens through a large cased opening into the exceptionally large living room, measuring 13 feet 6 inches by 27 feet and intended to be used as combination of living room and dining room. This room contains a rustic fireplace.

Our Windsor front door, glazed with leaded glass. Two sash on the right hand side of the living room, glazed with leaded glass. All the windows are Queen Anne style. Interior doors are five-cross panel with soft pine stiles and rails and yellow pine panels. Trim, such as baseboard, casing and molding, is clear yellow pine. Clear yellow pine flooring for entire house and porches.

A large overhanging roof serves for the porch roof and is supported by beams, thereby requiring no porch columns, leaving the front all open. Porch is 25 feet long and 8 feet 10 inches wide.

Built on a concrete foundation, frame construction, sided with narrow bevel edge cypress siding and has a cedar shingle roof.

Painted two coats outside; your choice of color. Varnish and wood filler for two coats of interior finish.

Excavated cellar, 12x24 feet, 7 feet high from floor to joists. Rooms on the main floor are 10 feet from floor to ceiling.

This house can be built on a lot 48 feet wide.

Complete Warm Air Heating Plant, for soft coal, extra	$ 59.83
Complete Warm Air Heating Plant, for hard coal, extra	63.07
Complete Steam Heating Plant, extra	143.97
Complete Hot Water Heating Plant, extra	186.67
Complete Plumbing Outfit, extra	120.21

SEARS, ROEBUCK AND CO.  **CHICAGO, ILLINOIS**

MODERN HOME No. 165

$1,362⁰⁰

For $1,362.00 we will furnish all the material to build this Six-Room House, consisting of Mill Work, Ceiling, Siding, Flooring, Finishing Lumber, Building Paper, Pipe, Gutter, Sash Weights, Hardware, Mantels, Painting Material, Lumber, Lath and Shingles. NO EXTRAS, as we guarantee enough material at the above price to build this house according to our plans.

By allowing a fair price for labor, cement, brick and plaster, which we do not furnish, this house can be built for about $2,640.00, including all material and labor.

For Our Offer of Free Plans See Page 3.

A COLONIAL one-story house particularly suited and arranged for a warm climate where a great deal of ventilation is desired. Large front porch, 40 feet by 9 feet 6 inches, with massive Colonial columns; also large rear porch. Large center hall, 10 feet by 32 feet 6 inches, with a door at each end. Doors from this hall lead to the two bedrooms, parlor and dining room. Double sliding doors between the two bedrooms and double sliding doors between dining room and parlor. You will notice by this arrangement and the ceilings being 12 feet high that the ventilation is perfect.

Front door and rear door at the opposite end of the hall, 3x7 feet, 1¾ inches thick, oak, glazed leaded glass. Interior doors are six-cross panel veneered oak with clear oak casing, base and molding. Clear yellow pine flooring for interior and porches. Mantel in hall, front bedroom, parlor and dining room. Outside blinds for all windows.

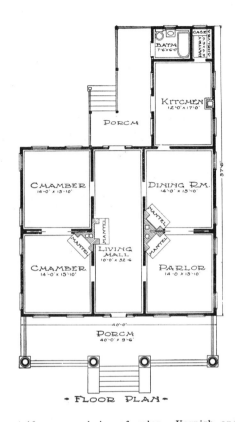

- FLOOR PLAN -

Painted two coats outside; your choice of color. Varnish and wood filler for interior finish.

This house is built on a concrete block foundation, frame construction, sided with narrow bevel edge cypress siding, gables sided with cedar shingles, and has cedar shingle roof.

Excavated basement under the entire house. Rooms on the main floor are 12 feet from floor to ceiling.

This house can be built on a lot 44 feet wide.

Complete Warm Air Heating Plant, for soft coal, extra	$134.72
Complete Warm Air Heating Plant, for hard coal, extra	139.67
Complete Steam Heating Plant, extra	228.31
Complete Hot Water Heating Plant, extra	267.82
Complete Plumbing Outfit, extra	100.48

SEARS, ROEBUCK AND CO.  **CHICAGO, ILLINOIS**

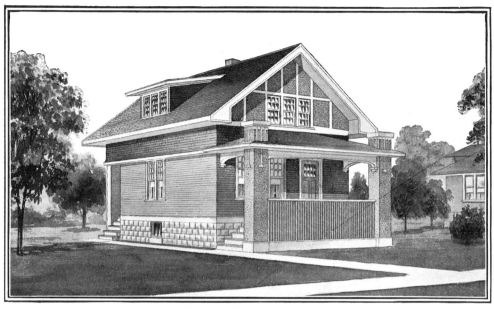

MODERN HOME No. 161

$902.00

For $902.00 we will furnish all the material to build this Seven-Room House, consisting of Mill Work, Ceiling, Siding, Flooring, Finishing Lumber, Building Paper, Pipe, Gutter, Sash Weights, Painting Material, Lumber, Lath and Shingles. **NO EXTRAS,** as we guarantee enough material at the above price to build this house according to our plans.

By allowing a fair price for labor, cement, brick and plaster, which we do not furnish, this house can be built for about $1,870.00, including all material and labor.

For Our Offer of Free Plans See Page 3.

A COTTAGE that cannot help but please you if you are looking for an up to date, modern cottage. It has the appearance of a high priced house, both in exterior and interior. Large front porch, 17x7 feet, with square stonekote columns with panel tops.

Queen Anne windows. Birch Craftsman front door. Two-panel veneered birch interior doors throughout the house. Birch trim. Oak flooring for the first floor; clear yellow pine flooring for the second floor and porches. Birch open stairway in the reception hall with inside cellar stairs directly under the main stairs. Cased opening between the hall and parlor. Large pantry and two closets on the first floor. Three bedrooms, four closets and bathroom on the second floor.

Built on a concrete block foundation, frame construction, sided with narrow bevel edge cypress siding to the belt course and cedar shingles above the belt course. Gables sided with stonekote. Cedar shingle roof with the exception of the dormers, which are covered with galvanized steel roofing.

Painted two coats outside; your choice of color. Varnish and wood filler for interior finish.

Excavated basement under the entire house, 7 feet from floor to joists, with cement floor. Rooms on the first floor are 9 feet from floor to ceiling; second floor, 8 feet 6 inches from floor to ceiling.

This house can be built on a lot 30 feet wide.

Complete Warm Air Heating Plant, for soft coal, extra	$ 77.24
Complete Warm Air Heating Plant, for hard coal, extra	80.18
Complete Steam Heating Plant, extra	147.54
Complete Hot Water Heating Plant, extra	188.22
Complete Plumbing Outfit, extra	120.87

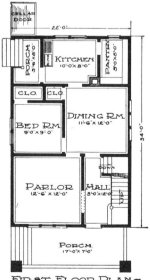

FIRST FLOOR PLAN

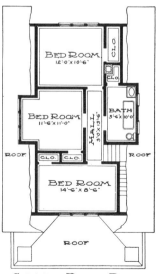

SECOND FLOOR PLAN

—37—

SEARS, ROEBUCK AND CO.  **CHICAGO, ILLINOIS**

$838^{00}

For $838.00 we will furnish all the material to build this Eight-Room Two-Story House, consisting of Lumber, Lath, Shingles, Mill Work, Flooring, Ceiling, Siding, Finishing Lumber, Building Paper, Pipe, Gutter, Sash Weights, Hardware and Painting Material. NO EXTRAS, as we guarantee enough material at the above price to build this house according to our plans.

By allowing a fair price for labor, concrete, brick and plaster, which we do not furnish, this house can be built for about $1,700.00, including all material and labor.

For Our Offer of Free Plans See Page 3.

THIS attractive two-story frame house of eight rooms is of a very simple pattern. Every inch of space has been used to the best advantage. The large triple window frame on the second story and the peculiar treatment of the roof give this house its attractive appearance. All windows in the front and sides are of Colonial pattern.

First Floor.

As one enters the front door of this house he immediately has a favorable impression from the large reception hall and the open stairway which leads to the second floor. The living room is directly off the reception hall and separated from the dining room by a cased opening. There is also a cased opening between the living room and dining room, and a large light pantry is conveniently situated between dining room and kitchen. The kitchen is 12 feet wide by 13 feet long and the entrance to the cellar is under the stairs leading to second floor. Hardwood flooring is furnished for the first floor.

Second Floor.

The second floor has four bedrooms of medium size, two closets and a nice bathroom. All interior doors for this house are of the five-cross panel design and made of clear yellow pine with yellow pine trim to match. Yellow pine flooring throughout for the second floor.

Built on a concrete foundation. Basement excavated and has cement floor. Cypress siding and cedar shingles.

Height of Ceilings.

Basement, 7 feet from floor to joists.
First and second floors, 8 feet from floor to ceiling.

This house can be built on a lot 30 feet wide.

Complete Warm Air Heating Plant, for soft coal, extra	$ 85.52
Complete Warm Air Heating Plant, for hard coal, extra	87.27
Complete Steam Heating Plant, extra	158.75
Complete Hot Water Heating Plant, extra	204.94
Complete Plumbing Outfit, extra	116.31

SEARS, ROEBUCK AND CO.  **CHICAGO, ILLINOIS**

MODERN HOME No. 180

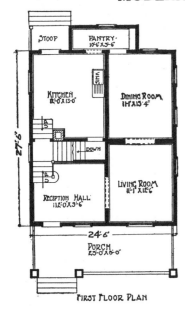

FIRST FLOOR PLAN

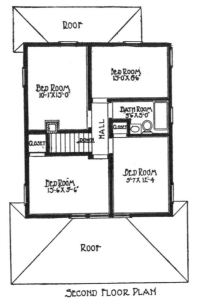

SECOND FLOOR PLAN

MODERN HOME No. 306

$1,512.00

For $1,512.00 we will furnish all the material to build this Eight-Room House, consisting of Mill Work, Ceiling, Siding, Flooring, Finishing Lumber, Bookcase, China Closet, Building Paper, Pipe, Gutter, Sash Weights, Hardware, Painting Material, Lumber, Lath and Shingles. **NO EXTRAS**, as we guarantee enough material at the above price to build this house according to our plans.

By allowing a fair price for labor, stone, cement, brick and plaster, which we do not furnish, this house can be built for about $2,970.00, including all material and labor.

For Our Offer of Free Plans See Page 3.

A LARGE modern residence with very large front porch, 46 feet long by 8 feet wide, with Colonial columns. Superba front door, 3x7 feet, 1¾ inches thick, veneered oak, glazed bevel plate glass. Julien dining room door, glazed with lace design glass. Leaded Crystal windows for front of reception hall, library, stair landing and dining room bay. For attic, Queen Anne sash.

Large reception hall opening directly into the library with colonnade opening between them. A well designed open stairway leading to the second floor.

The kitchen stairs leading to the landing of the main stairs enable one to go to the second floor from either the front hall or kitchen. This stair landing contains a long seat on the three sides of the bay, with a large mirror on the entry side of the landing bay which reflects directly into the reception hall.

Six-cross panel oak interior doors for the first floor with clear oak trim, molding, colonnade and open stair material; oak floor. Second floor finished with five-cross panel solid clear yellow pine doors and yellow pine trim, with clear yellow pine flooring for the second floor and porches. Dining room contains a china closet. The library has built in bookcase with leaded glass doors.

Painted two coats outside; your choice of color. Varnish and wood filler for interior finish.

Built on a stone foundation, frame construction, sided with narrow bevel edge cypress siding and has cedar shingle roof.

Excavated basement under the entire house, 7 feet 2 inches from floor to joists, with cement floor. First floor, 9 feet 2 inches from floor to ceiling; second floor, 8 feet from floor to ceiling.

This house can be built on a lot 48 feet wide.

Complete Warm Air Heating Plant, for soft coal, extra	$ 92.14
Complete Warm Air Heating Plant, for hard coal, extra	94.87
Complete Steam Heating Plant, extra	202.04
Complete Hot Water Heating Plant, extra	248.32
Complete Plumbing Outfit, extra	147.37

SEARS, ROEBUCK AND CO.  **CHICAGO, ILLINOIS**

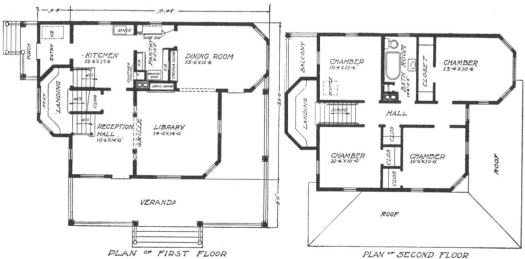

PLAN OF FIRST FLOOR   PLAN OF SECOND FLOOR

MODERN HOME No. 102   Trimmed Clear Nona White Pine.
MODERN HOME No. 102½   Oak Finish First Floor.

$1,161.00

For $1,161.00 we will furnish all the material to build this Ten-Room House, consisting of Mill Work, Flooring, Ceiling, Siding, Finishing Lumber, Building Paper, Pipe, Gutter, Sash Weights, China Closet, Hardware, Painting Material, Lumber, Lath and Shingles. NO EXTRAS, as we guarantee enough material at the above price to build this house according to our plans.

By allowing a fair price for labor, stone, brick and plaster, which we do not furnish, this house can be built for about $2,300.00, including all material and labor.

For Our Offer of Free Plans See Page 3.

A SQUARE house is always desirable. It is easy to build as the design is simple and requires less mechanical labor than other styles of architecture. It affords a great deal of room and has a good appearance for the amount of money invested. This house has ten good size conveniently arranged rooms. Front hall has sliding doors leading to the living room; also sliding doors to the parlor. Grille between the parlor and dining room. Kitchen connected with the dining room and large butler's pantry. Open stairway leading to the second floor. Four large bedrooms with two windows in each room. Large size bathroom and four closets on the second floor.

Queen Anne window in the hall on the second floor; leaded glass window for the living room and parlor. Metropole front door, glazed with leaded glass. All interior doors are five-cross panel with soft pine stiles and rails, yellow pine panels. Clear pine trim throughout. Clear yellow pine flooring for the entire house and 1⅛-inch clear fir flooring for porches.

Painted two coats on the outside. Varnish and wood filler for two coats of interior finish.

Built on a stone foundation, frame construction, sided with narrow bevel edge clear cypress siding and has *A* cedar shingle roof. Large front porch, 26 feet 6 inches wide by 6 feet 3 inches deep; rear porch, 15 feet 6 inches long by 4 feet wide.

Excavated basement under the entire house, 7 feet 2 inches from floor to joists. Rooms on the first floor, 9 feet 3 inches from floor to ceiling; second floor, 8 feet 4 inches from floor to ceiling.

This house can be furnished with clear oak stairs and trim and oak flooring on the first floor for $64.00 extra. If you want it finished this way, order plans for Modern Home No. 102½.

This house is 32 feet wide by 36 feet long and can be built on a lot 36 feet wide.

Complete Warm Air Heating Plant, for soft coal, extra	$ 80.32
Complete Warm Air Heating Plant, for hard coal, extra	82.35
Complete Steam Heating Plant, extra	200.98
Complete Hot Water Heating Plant, extra	244.97
Complete Plumbing Outfit, extra	118.25

FIRST·FLOOR·PLAN.

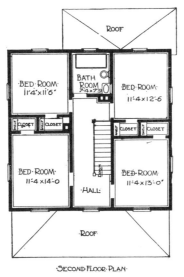

SECOND·FLOOR·PLAN.

—40—

SEARS, ROEBUCK AND CO.      **CHICAGO, ILLINOIS**

MODERN HOME No. 127

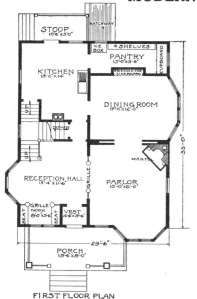

FIRST FLOOR PLAN

SECOND FLOOR PLAN

$1,538.⁰⁰

For $1,538.00 we will furnish all the material to build this Eight-Room House, consisting of Mill Work, Ceiling, Siding, Flooring, Finishing Lumber, Building Paper, Pipe, Gutter, Sash Weights, Mantel, Hardware, Painting Material, Lumber, Lath and Shingles. NO EXTRAS, as we guarantee enough material at the above price to build this house according to our plans.

By allowing a fair price for labor, cement, brick and plaster, which we do not furnish, this house can be built for about $3,050.00, including all material and labor.

For Our Offer of Free Plans See Page 3.

A STRICTLY modern residence, conveniently arranged. Has a large reception hall, 15 feet 4 inches by 11 feet 6 inches, separated from the parlor by a pair of colonnades and also separated from the nook, which is often used as a reading room, by a pair of colonnades. This nook has a seat built in on each end. Double sliding doors between parlor and dining room. Dining room has a sideboard built into the wall. A mantel in the parlor. Open oak staircase in the reception hall. Every part of this house is well lighted and ventilated by means of two or more windows in each room.

Ottawa front door glazed with leaded art glass. Interior doors on first floor, six-cross panel oak veneered; five-cross panel solid yellow pine doors on second floor. Oak trim, such as casing, baseboard and molding, throughout the first floor; second floor trimmed clear yellow pine baseboard, casing and molding. Oak flooring for main rooms on first floor; maple flooring for kitchen and pantry; clear yellow pine flooring for the second floor and porches. Note the stairs leading from the kitchen, which connect with the main stairs enabling one to go to the second floor from either the reception hall or kitchen.

Painted two coats outside; your choice of color. Varnish and wood filler for interior finish.

Built on a concrete block foundation, frame construction. Sided with narrow bevel edge cypress siding and has cedar shingle roof. Outside blinds for all windows except attic.

Excavated basement under the entire house, 7 feet 4 inches from floor to joists. First floor, 9 feet 6 inches from floor to ceiling; second floor, 8 feet 6 inches from floor to ceiling.

This house can be built on a lot 36 feet wide.

Complete Warm Air Heating Plant, for soft coal, extra	$101.57
Complete Warm Air Heating Plant, for hard coal, extra	103.72
Complete Steam Heating Plant, extra	204.13
Complete Hot Water Heating Plant, extra	259.07
Complete Plumbing Outfit, extra	128.12

SEARS, ROEBUCK AND CO.  **CHICAGO, ILLINOIS**

$1,625.00

For $1,625.00 we will furnish all the material to build this Ten-Room House, consisting of Mill Work, Siding, Flooring, Ceiling, Finishing Lumber, Building Paper, Pipe, Gutter, Sash Weights, Hardware, Painting Material, Lumber, Lath and Shingles. NO EXTRAS, as we guarantee enough material at the above price to build this house according to our plans.

By allowing a fair price for labor, cement, brick and plaster, which we do not furnish, this house can be built for about $3,345.00, including all material and labor.

For Our Offer of Free Plans See Page 3.

A GOOD substantial design, yet constructed with a view to economy and affording a great deal of room. It has a large front porch, 7 feet wide by 24 feet long, with balcony over part of it, 8 feet 6 inches by 12 feet; door leads to the balcony from the front chamber on the second floor. Ionic columns on the front porch put up in pairs. Crescent cottage windows glazed with colored leaded art glass for the front of the parlor, bay window in the sitting room, large window in the dining room, and bay window in the side chamber on the second floor. Veneered oak front door, leaded art glass. Large reception hall with oak open stairway with closet directly under it. Door between the reception hall and the dining room; door between sitting room and reception hall. Grille between reception hall and parlor; cased opening between sitting room and parlor; mantel in the parlor. Large kitchen, pantry and storeroom on the first floor. Rear stairway leads to the second floor from the kitchen; cellar stairs directly underneath with a landing even with the grade line with an outside door opening to it. Second floor has three large bedrooms and two medium size ones; bathroom and five closets.

Six-cross panel oak veneered interior doors for the first floor with clear oak trim and molding. Plate rail for the dining room. Yellow pine interior doors and trim for the entire second floor. Oak flooring for the main rooms on the first floor; maple flooring for pantry and kitchen; clear yellow pine flooring for the entire second floor and porches.

Painted two coats outside. Varnish and wood filler for two coats of interior finish.

Built on a concrete block foundation, frame construction, sided with narrow bevel edge cypress siding and has cedar shingle roof.

Excavated basement under the entire house, 7 feet 4 inches from floor to joists. First floor, 9 feet 6 inches from floor to ceiling; second floor, 9 feet from floor to ceiling.

This house can be built on a lot 35 feet wide.

Complete Warm Air Heating Plant, for soft coal, extra	$121.81
Complete Warm Air Heating Plant, for hard coal, extra	125.17
Complete Steam Heating Plant, extra	236.86
Complete Hot Water Heating Plant, extra	270.72
Complete Plumbing Outfit, extra	144.75

MODERN HOME No. 119

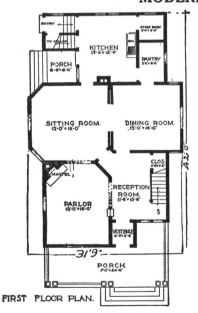

FIRST FLOOR PLAN.

SECOND FLOOR PLAN.

—42—

SEARS, ROEBUCK AND CO.  CHICAGO, ILLINOIS

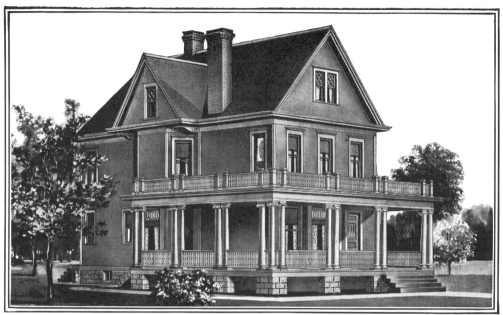

MODERN HOME No. 120

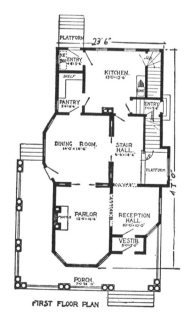

FIRST FLOOR PLAN

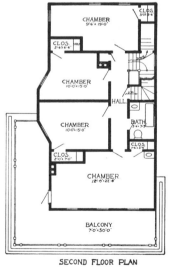

SECOND FLOOR PLAN

—43—

$1,660.00

For $1,660.00 we will furnish all the material to build this Nine-Room House, consisting of Mill Work, Siding, Flooring, Ceiling, Finishing Lumber, Building Paper, Pipe, Gutter, Sash Weights, Hardware, Mantel, Painting Material, Lumber, Lath and Shingles. NO EXTRAS, as we guarantee enough material at the above price to build this house according to our plans.

By allowing a fair price for labor, cement, brick and plaster, which we do not furnish, this house can be built for about $3,243.00, including all material and labor.

For Our Offer of Free Plans See Page 3.

A CITY, country or suburban residence. It has a large front porch, 50 feet long by 7 feet wide, with a balcony porch. Colonial porch columns placed in pairs, and in groups of three at the corners, and with newels on the balcony directly over the columns add to the general beauty of this design.

The reception hall is separated from the stair hall with a cased opening between them. Grille between the reception hall and parlor. Double sliding doors between parlor and dining room; double sliding doors between stair hall and dining room. Large kitchen and pantry. Grade entrance on the right hand side leading to the kitchen and also down to the basement under the main stairs. Rear stairs from the kitchen leading to the second floor, joining the main stairs at the second landing; attic stairs directly over the main stairs. Mantel and fireplace in the parlor. Plate rail in the dining room. One extraordinarily large front chamber on the second floor and three other good size bedrooms and four closets.

Hamilton design veneered oak front door glazed with leaded glass. Inside doors for first floor are six-cross panel veneered oak, with oak trim and oak open stairway. Five-cross panel clear yellow pine doors and yellow pine trim for the second floor. Oak flooring for the main rooms on the first floor; maple flooring for the kitchen and pantry; clear yellow pine flooring for the second floor and porches.

Painted two coats outside; your choice of color. Varnish and wood filler for interior finish.

Built on a concrete block foundation, frame construction, sided with narrow bevel edge cypress siding and has a cedar shingle roof.

Excavated basement under the entire house, 7 feet 4 inches from floor to joists. First floor, 9 feet from floor to ceiling; second floor, 8 feet 6 inches from floor to ceiling; large attic, 7 feet from floor to collar beam.

This house can be built on a lot 36 feet wide.

Complete Warm Air Heating Plant, for soft coal, extra	$103.86
Complete Warm Air Heating Plant, for hard coal, extra	106.34
Complete Steam Heating Plant, extra	180.15
Complete Hot Water Heating Plant, extra	239.32
Complete Plumbing Outfit, extra	150.00

SEARS, ROEBUCK AND CO.  QUALITY GUARANTEED **CHICAGO, ILLINOIS**

MODERN HOME No. 190

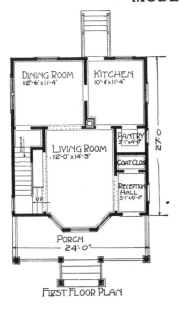

FIRST FLOOR PLAN

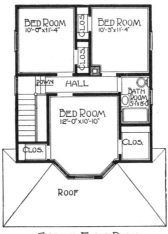

SECOND FLOOR PLAN

$828.00

For $828.00 we will furnish all the material to build this Six-Room House, consisting of Lumber, Lath, Shingles, Mill Work, Flooring, Ceiling, Siding, Finishing Lumber, Building Paper, Pipe, Gutter, Sash Weights, Hardware and Painting Material. NO EXTRAS, as we guarantee enough material at the above price to build this house according to our plans.

By allowing a fair price for labor, cement, brick and plaster, which we do not furnish, this house can be built for about $1,700.00, including all material and labor.

For Our Offer of Free Plans See Page 3.

THIS comfortable little home is pleasing and homelike. It has a large bay window on both the first and second floors. The porch is 24 feet wide by 7 feet 6 inches deep. This house has a small reception hall 5 feet 1 inch wide by 6 feet 11 inches long. Directly off this reception hall is the large roomy coat closet. A cased opening separates the reception hall from the living room. The living room is 14 feet 3 inches long by 12 feet wide. By referring to the floor plan you will note that the left hand side of the living room has a large cased opening 10 feet wide by 7 feet high which opens onto the stairway leading to the second floor. The dining room and kitchen are both fair size rooms; the kitchen has a pantry 4 feet by 5 feet 1 inch in which a pantry case is built. All rooms on the first floor will be perfectly cool on the hottest days, the ventilation being perfect. The entrance to the basement is through the dining room, basement stairs being immediately under the stairs leading from the first floor to the second floor.

First Floor.

Front door made of clear white pine, 1¾ inches thick, glazed with bevel plate glass. Inside doors are of the five-cross panel design, made of the best quality yellow pine with yellow pine trim to match. Yellow pine flooring for first floor.

Second Floor.

Stairs from first floor lead to hall on second floor, the entrance to each of the three bedrooms being off this hall. Each of the two rear bedrooms has a clothes closet; the front bedroom has two large clothes closets. All doors, trim and flooring are made of yellow pine, the doors being five-cross panel design.

Built on a concrete block foundation with basement under the entire house. We furnish cypress siding and cedar shingles, framing timbers of best quality yellow pine. Basement has cement floor.

Height of Ceilings.

Basement, 7 feet from floor to joists.
First floor, 9 feet from floor to ceiling.
Second floor, 8 feet 6 inches from floor to ceiling.
Painted with two coats of best quality paint outside, varnish and wood filler for interior finish.

This house can be built on a lot 28 feet wide.

Complete Warm Air Heating Plant, for soft coal, extra	$ 70.88
Complete Warm Air Heating Plant, for hard coal, extra	74.18
Complete Steam Heating Plant, extra	147.40
Complete Hot Water Heating Plant, extra	183.69
Complete Plumbing Outfit, extra	117.96

SEARS, ROEBUCK AND CO.  **CHICAGO, ILLINOIS**

MODERN HOME No. 156

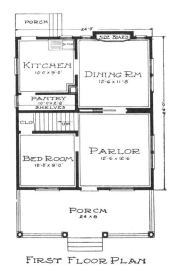

FIRST FLOOR PLAN   SECOND FLOOR PLAN

$723.00

For $723.00 we will furnish all the material to build this Six-Room Bungalow, consisting of Lumber, Lath, Shingles, Mill Work, Flooring, Ceiling, Siding, Finishing Lumber, Building Paper, Pipe, Gutter, Sash Weights, Hardware and Painting Material. NO EXTRAS, as we guarantee enough material at the above price to build this house according to our plans.

By allowing a fair price for labor, cement, brick and plaster, which we do not furnish, this house can be built for about $1,500.00, including all material and labor.

For Our Offer of Free Plans See Page 3.

A MODERN six-room bungalow of frame construction, built along plain lines of good materials, yet at a price that is within reach of every purse. Every inch of space is used to the best advantage, the rooms being large in proportion to the exterior measurements of the house. The numerous windows, some of which are double, make every room light and airy. To bring out the bungalow effect our architect has designed a long sloping roof extending over the porch, and ornamented same by an attractive shingled dormer with four windows. The porch extends across the front of the house, measuring 24 feet long by 8 feet wide. Colonial porch columns and balusters are used with pleasing effect.

First Floor.

The front entrance leads directly into a large parlor, 12 feet 6 inches by 12 feet 6 inches, and separated from the dining room, which is arranged directly in the rear, with sliding door. The dining room, measuring 12 feet 6 inches by 11 feet 8 inches, has plate rail and buffet or china cabinet with small windows placed above plate rail at both sides of the cabinet and directly opposite the large sliding doors, being plainly visible from the parlor. Directly off the dining room is located the kitchen with large pantry, also sink, which is placed directly in front of rear window. Glazed sash door leads from kitchen to back stoop. Directly off from parlor is a door leading to bedroom 9 feet by 10 feet with closet. This room can be used as a library or music room. The stairway leads from parlor to the second floor.

Second Floor.

Directly at the head of the stairs on the second floor is a hall which leads to front bedroom, size, 11 feet 6 inches by 12 feet 6 inches, with closet, and rear bedroom 8 feet 6 inches by 13 feet 9 inches, with large closet. At the head of the stairs is a door leading to bathroom 8 feet 9 inches by 8 feet 6 inches.

For the front door we furnish a heavy 1¾-inch door with etched design glass. Parlor and front bedroom, or library, have large cottage windows and double windows on the side. The interior doors are made of yellow pine and have five-cross panels. All trim, including baseboard, casings, interior molding and stair material, is made of yellow pine. Clear yellow pine flooring is used in all rooms and on porch. No. 1 yellow pine ceiling for porch.

Built on concrete block foundation. Sided with narrow bevel edge cypress siding and cedar shingles on the sides of dormer and on roof. All framing material, including joists, studding, etc., made from No. 1 yellow pine.

Height of Ceilings.

First floor, 9 feet from floor to ceiling.
Second floor, 8 feet from floor to ceiling.
We furnish two coats of paint for outside, your choice of color. Varnish and wood filler for interior finish.

This house can be built on a lot 27 feet 6 inches wide.

Complete Warm Air Heating Plant, for soft coal, extra	$ 81.20
Complete Warm Air Heating Plant, for hard coal, extra	83.64
Complete Steam Heating Plant, extra	141.73
Complete Hot Water Heating Plant, extra	169.97
Complete Plumbing Outfit, extra	117.02

SEARS, ROEBUCK AND CO.  **CHICAGO, ILLINOIS**

$1,123.00

For $1,123.00 we will furnish all the material to build this Eight-Room House, consisting of Mill Work, Ceiling, Siding, Flooring, Finishing Lumber, Building Paper, Pipe, Gutter, Sash Weights, Hardware, Painting Material, Lumber, Lath and Shingles. NO EXTRAS, as we guarantee enough material at the above price to build this house according to our plans.

By allowing a fair price for labor, cement, brick and plaster, which we do not furnish, this house can be built for about $2,345.00, including all material and labor.

For Our Offer of Free Plans See Page 3.

A CONVENIENTLY arranged house with four large rooms on the first floor and four on the second floor with closet for each bedroom and one closet opening into the stair hall on the second floor. Inside cellar stairs leading to the side entrance and also continuing down to the basement directly under the main stairs, thereby using but very little space for the two stairways. Large front porch 24 feet long extending almost clear across the front of the house.

The front door is our Circe design, veneered oak, glazed with colored leaded art glass. The interior doors on the first floor are six-cross panel veneered oak, and all trim, such as baseboard, casing and molding, is clear plain sawed oak. The doors on the second floor are five-cross panel solid yellow pine with clear yellow pine trim. Open oak staircase. Clear yellow pine flooring throughout the entire house and porches.

Paint for two coats of exterior work; your choice of color. Varnish and wood filler for two coats of interior finish.

Built on a concrete block foundation and is of frame construction. The first story is sided with stonekote, more commonly known as cement plaster; the second story is sided with narrow bevel edge cypress siding. Has cedar shingle roof.

An excavated basement under the entire house, 7 feet 2 inches from floor to joists. Rooms on the first floor are 9 feet 2 inches from floor to ceiling; second floor, 9 feet from floor to ceiling.

This house is 28 feet wide by 38 feet 6 inches long and can be built on a lot 32 feet wide

Complete Warm Air Heating Plant, for soft coal, extra	$100.22
Complete Warm Air Heating Plant, for hard coal, extra	102.37
Complete Steam Heating Plant, extra	193.47
Complete Hot Water Heating Plant, extra	233.92
Complete Plumbing Outfit, extra	128.00

SEARS, ROEBUCK AND CO.  **CHICAGO, ILLINOIS**

MODERN HOME No. 111

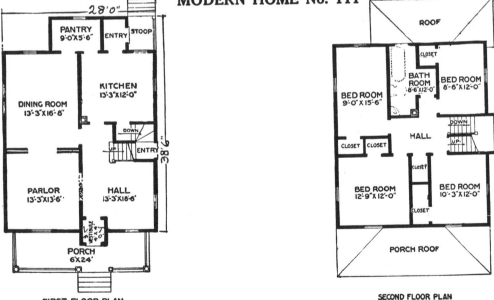

FIRST FLOOR PLAN

SECOND FLOOR PLAN

$753.00

MODERN HOME No. 167

For $753.00 we will furnish all the material to build this Eight-Room House, consisting of Mill Work, Flooring, Ceiling, Siding, Finishing Lumber, Building Paper, Pipe, Gutter, Sash Weights, Hardware, Painting Material, Lumber, Lath and Shingles. **NO EXTRAS**, as we guarantee enough material at the above price to build this house according to our plans.

By allowing a fair price for labor, cement, brick and plaster, which we do not furnish, this house can be built for about $1,573.00, including all material and labor.

For Our Offer of Free Plans See Page 3.

A WELL proportioned house which affords a great deal of room at a low cost. Large front porch, 21 feet 6 inches long by 8 feet wide, with Colonial columns. Bay window in the dining room and parlor. An octagon tower on the second floor, making it suitable for a corner lot. Crystal leaded front window in the parlor. Colored leaded art glass sash for the hall, with marginal light attic sash. Every room in the house is perfectly lighted and well ventilated by large windows. The reception hall contains an open staircase with a cased opening between it and the parlor, and another cased opening leading to the dining room. A door also opens from the reception hall directly into the kitchen. Inside cellar stairs directly under the main stairs and also an outside stairway under the rear porch. When reaching the second floor landing you are within a very few feet of the entrance to the three bedrooms or bathroom. By this you will notice there is no waste space whatever.

Dublin front door, 3x7 feet, glazed with bevel plate glass. Interior yellow pine doors for both first and second floor, with clear yellow pine trim, such as casing, baseboard and molding. Clear yellow pine flooring for both floors and porches.

Painted two coats outside; color to suit. Varnish and wood filler for two coats of interior finish.

Built on a concrete block foundation, frame construction, sided with narrow bevel cypress edge siding and has a cedar shingle roof.

Excavated basement under the entire house, 7 feet from floor to joists, with cement floor. First floor, 9 feet from floor to ceiling; second floor, 8 feet from floor to ceiling.

This house can be built on a lot 28 feet wide.

Complete Warm Air Heating Plant, for soft coal, extra	$ 78.05
Complete Warm Air Heating Plant, for hard coal, extra	80.54
Complete Steam Heating Plant, extra	173.49
Complete Hot Water Heating Plant, extra	206.72
Complete Plumbing Outfit, extra	117.27

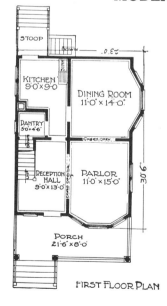

FIRST FLOOR PLAN

SECOND FLOOR PLAN

—47—

SEARS, ROEBUCK AND CO.  **CHICAGO, ILLINOIS**

MODERN HOME No. 188.

FIRST FLOOR PLAN

DINING ROOM
11'-1"x16'-1"

KITCHEN
11'-0"x11'-0"

STOOP

DOWN

PANTRY
7'-1"x5'-1"

LIVING ROOM
11'-1"x13'-0"

RECEPTION HALL
11'-0"x13'-0"

PORCH
23'-6"x8'-0"

23'-6"

30'-6"

SECOND FLOOR PLAN

BED ROOM
14'-1"x13'-0"

BATHROOM
8'-0"x11'-0"

DOWN

CLOSET CLOSET

HALL
8'-0"x9'-0"

BED ROOM
11'-1"x13'-0"

BED ROOM
11'-0"x8'-8"

ROOF

926<u>00</u>

For $926.00 we will furnish all the material to build this Eight-Room House, consisting of Lumber, Lath, Shingles, Mill Work, Flooring, Ceiling, Siding, Finishing Lumber, Building Paper, Pipe, Gutter, Sash Weights, Hardware and Painting Material. NO EXTRAS, as we guarantee enough material at the above price to build this house according to our plans.

By allowing a fair price for labor, cement, brick and plaster, which we do not furnish, this house can be built for about $1,850.00, including all material and labor.

For Our Offer of Free Plans See Page 3.

THIS house is very similar to our Modern Home No. 167, shown on page 47, excepting that it is 1½ feet wider and 2 feet longer. Our customers consider this house an ideal home as well as a good investment, having the appearance of a house costing $2,500.00 to build.

The front porch is 23 feet 6 inches by 8 feet, reception hall is 11 feet by 13 feet and has an open stairway leading to the second floor. The cased opening separates the reception hall from the parlor. The parlor or living room is 13 feet long by 11 feet 1 inch wide. The dining room is also a good size room, being 16 feet 1 inch by 11 feet 1 inch and has a large bay window extending almost the entire length of the room. Kitchen has a good size pantry. The stairway leading to the basement has its entrance in the pantry.

First Floor.

The front door is of white pine, 1¾ inches thick, glazed with bevel plate glass. Doors are of the four-panel design, made of the best quality yellow pine. All floors and inside trim are a clear grade of yellow pine.

Second Floor.

On the second floor there are two large bedrooms, each having large clothes closet, and one small bedroom. Also a good size bathroom, size 8 feet wide by 11 feet long.

Stairs from first floor lead to the hall on the second floor, from which the bathroom or any of the three bedrooms may be entered. All doors, trim and floors are of the best quality yellow pine.

Built on a brick foundation and excavated under entire house. We furnish clear cypress siding and cedar shingles; framing timbers of the best quality yellow pine. Leaded crystal glass front window. All windows "A" quality double strength glass.

Height of Ceiling.

Basement, 7 feet from floor to joists.
First floor, 9 feet from floor to ceiling.
Second floor, 8 feet from floor to ceiling.
Painted with two coats of the best paint outside, varnish and wood filler for interior finish.

This house can be built on a lot 30 feet wide.

Complete Warm Air Heating Plant, for soft coal, extra	$ 82.07
Complete Warm Air Heating Plant, for hard coal, extra	84.08
Complete Steam Heating Plant, extra	185.35
Complete Hot Water Heating Plant, extra	204.72
Complete Plumbing Outfit, extra	124.10

SEARS, ROEBUCK AND CO.  **CHICAGO, ILLINOIS**

MODERN HOME No. 133

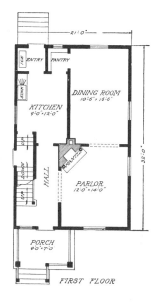

FIRST FLOOR

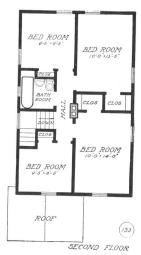

SECOND FLOOR

$759 00

For $759.00 we will furnish all the material to build this Eight-Room House, consisting of Mill Work, Flooring, Ceiling, Siding, Finishing Lumber, Building Paper, Pipe, Gutter, Sash Weights, Hardware, Mantel, Painting Material, Lumber, Lath and Shingles. NO EXTRAS, as we guarantee enough material at the above price to build this house according to our plans.

By allowing a fair price for labor, cement, brick and plaster, which we do not furnish, this house can be built for about $1,500.00, including all material and labor.

For Our Offer of Free Plans See Page 3.

A SIMPLE and well constructed house which if built according to our plans and with our material will prove a very good paying investment, as it affords a great deal of room for the small amount of money. Fair size porch, 7x9 feet, with Colonial columns. Queen Anne windows in the front and leaded Crystal window in the parlor. Stair hall with door leading to the kitchen. Cased opening between the parlor and dining room. Grade entrance on the left side of the house leading to the kitchen, also down to the basement. Mantel and fireplace in the parlor. Four good size rooms on the second floor with bathroom and four closets.

Our Polk design front door. Five-cross panel yellow pine inside doors with clear yellow pine molding and trim throughout the house, and clear yellow pine stairs. Clear yellow pine flooring for the entire house and porches.

Painted two coats outside; your choice of color. Varnish and wood filler for interior finish.

Built on a concrete foundation, frame construction, sided with narrow bevel edge cypress siding to the belt course and sided with cedar shingles above the belt course, and has cedar shingle roof.

Excavated basement under the entire house, 6 feet 6 inches from floor to joists. First floor, 9 feet from floor to ceiling; second floor, 8 feet 6 inches from floor to ceiling.

This house can be built on a lot 25 feet wide.

Complete Warm Air Heating Plant, for soft coal, extra	$ 86.20
Complete Warm Air Heating Plant, for hard coal, extra	88.49
Complete Steam Heating Plant, extra	168.10
Complete Hot Water Heating Plant, extra	200.32
Complete Plumbing Outfit, extra	108.00

SEARS, ROEBUCK AND CO.  **CHICAGO, ILLINOIS**

MODERN HOME No. 226

$822⁰⁰

For $822.00 we will furnish all the material to build this Seven-Room House, consisting of Lumber, Lath, Shingles, Mill Work, Flooring, Ceiling, Siding, Finishing Lumber, Building Paper, Pipe, Gutter, Sash Weights, Brick Mantel, Hardware and Painting Material. NO EXTRAS, as we guarantee enough material at the above price to build this house according to our plans.

By allowing a fair price for labor, cement, brick and plaster, which we do not furnish, this house can be built for about $1,700.00, including all material and labor.

For Our Offer of Free Plans See Page 3.

A PLAIN gable roof house of good appearance, having seven rooms and bath, built along plain and simple lines, but with many attractive features. Another combination may be had by finishing the first story with siding instead of the stonekote. This will not change the cost of the completed building to any great extent. The large front porch can be screened in at a small cost and used as a sleeping porch. The side entrance is a practical feature.

The side entrance opens into the reception hall which is separated from the living room by a large cased opening. The living room is 21 feet long by 13 feet deep and has a large open brick fireplace. The entrance to front porch is through a pair of French doors, on both sides of which are French casement sash. The dining room is 13 feet 2 inches by 11 feet with cased opening to reception hall and door to kitchen. A good size pantry with a pantry case. Has inside stairway to cellar.

First Floor.

Main entrance door is made of white pine, 1¾ inches thick, glazed with a long light of bevel plate glass. The rear door is also of white pine, 1¾ inches thick; is glazed with "A" quality clear glass. Interior doors are clear yellow pine, with five-cross panels, and clear yellow pine trim to match. Floors are also of clear yellow pine.

Second Floor.

Stairs from the first floor to the second floor are clear yellow pine and lead into a small hall, from which any one of the four bedrooms or bathroom may be reached. All bedrooms have clothes closets. All rooms light and airy. Doors clear yellow pine, five-cross panel. Clear yellow pine trim and floors.

Built on a concrete foundation, excavated under entire house. We furnish cedar shingles and No. 1 yellow pine framing timbers.

Height of Ceilings.

Basement has cement floor and is 7 feet from floor to joists.
First floor is 9 feet from floor to ceiling. Second floor is 8 feet 6 inches from floor to ceiling.
Stain and paint furnished for the outside, varnish and wood filler for the interior finish.

This house can be built on a lot 32 feet wide.

Complete Warm Air Heating Plant, for soft coal, extra	$ 90.21
Complete Warm Air Heating Plant, for hard coal, extra	92.22
Complete Steam Heating Plant, extra	158.50
Complete Hot Water Heating Plant, extra	197.72
Complete Plumbing Outfit, extra	125.63

FIRST FLOOR PLAN

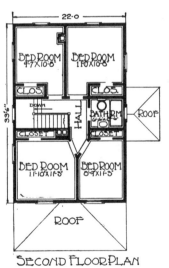

SECOND FLOOR PLAN

—50—

SEARS, ROEBUCK AND CO.  **CHICAGO, ILLINOIS**

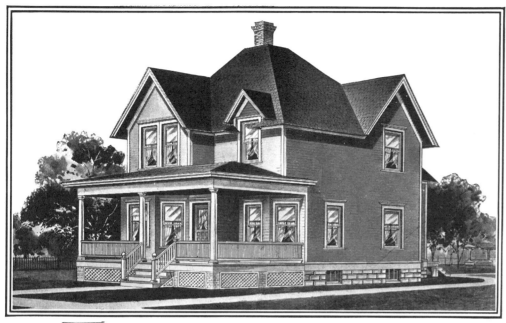

MODERN HOME No. 114

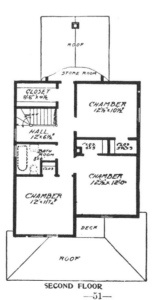

FIRST FLOOR

26'0"

46'0"

KITCHEN 11'x11½'

PANTRY 12'x4½'

DINING RM 12'9"x12'

CHAMBER 12'x10'

SITTING ROOM 12'6"x13'

PARLOR 12'x14'

VEST 3'6"x

PORCH 24'x7'

SECOND FLOOR

ROOF

STORE ROOM

CLOSET 9'6"x4½'

HALL 12'x6½'

BATH ROOM 8½'x

CHAMBER 12½'x10½'

CHAMBER 12½'x12'

CHAMBER 12'x11½'

DECK

ROOF

—51—

$958⁰⁰

For $958.00 we will furnish all the material to build this Eight-Room House, consisting of Mill Work, Ceiling, Siding, Flooring, Finishing Lumber, Building Paper, Pipe, Gutter, Sash Weights, Hardware, Painting Material, Lumber, Lath and Shingles. **NO EXTRAS,** as we guarantee enough material at the above price to build this house according to our plans.

By allowing a fair price for labor, cement, brick and plaster, which we do not furnish, this house can be built for about $2,000.00, including all material and labor.

For Our Offer of Free Plans See Page 3.

A HIGH CLASS modern type of residence that can be built at surprisingly low cost. Has large front porch, 24 feet long. Combination of hip and gable roof and Colonial porch columns. A pair of double sliding doors between the sitting room and dining room. A large cased opening between parlor and sitting room. Chamber on the first floor with door leading to the sitting room, one leading to the dining room and one leading to the pantry, which leads to the kitchen. Stairs from the dining room to the second floor, and directly under the main stairs is a cellar stair to the basement. Three large bedrooms on the second floor with closets; bathroom and stair hall.

Cass front door, clear five-cross panel solid yellow pine interior doors for both first and second floors. Clear yellow pine casing, baseboard and trim throughout the entire house. Clear yellow pine flooring throughout the entire house and porches.

Built on a concrete block foundation, frame construction, sided with narrow bevel edge cypress siding and has cedar shingle roof.

Painted two coats outside; your choice of color. Varnish and wood filler for interior finish.

Excavated basement under the entire house, 7 feet from floor to joists. First floor, 9 feet 2 inches from floor to ceiling; second floor, 8 feet from floor to ceiling.

This house measures 26x46 feet and can be built on a lot 30 feet wide.

Complete Warm Air Heating Plant, for soft coal, extra .... $ 93.34
Complete Warm Air Heating Plant, for hard coal, extra 95.39
Complete Steam Heating Plant, extra 151.80
Complete Hot Water Heating Plant, extra 199.39
Complete Plumbing Outfit, extra 87.96

SEARS, ROEBUCK AND CO.  **CHICAGO, ILLINOIS**

MODERN HOME No. 112

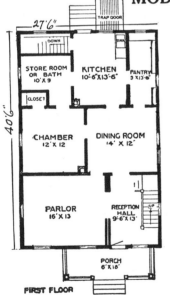

FIRST FLOOR

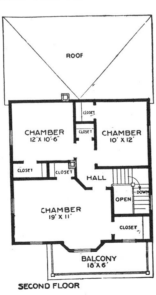

SECOND FLOOR

—52—

$1,031.00

For $1,031.00 we will furnish all the material to build this large Eight-Room House, consisting of Mill Work, Flooring, Ceiling, Siding, Finishing Lumber, Building Paper, Eaves Trough, Hardware, Painting Material, Lumber, Lath and Shingles. NO EXTRAS, as we guarantee enough material at the above price to build this house according to our plans.

By allowing a fair price for labor, cement, brick and plaster, which we do not furnish, this house can be built for about $2,170.00, including all material and labor.

For Our Offer of Free Plans See Page 3.

ROOMS are conveniently arranged. Large parlor, 16 feet wide by 13 feet long, connected with the reception hall with a 7-foot sliding door. Large dining room, chamber, bathroom and kitchen. Oak open stairway in the reception hall. Three large bedrooms on the second floor. Front bedroom is 19x11 feet, with a bay window opening out to the balcony over the front porch. Balcony is 18x6 feet.

Majestic front door glazed with bevel plate glass. The inside doors for both first and second floors are clear solid yellow pine, five-cross panel, with clear yellow pine trim, such as baseboard, casing and molding for both first and second floors. Clear yellow pine flooring for the entire house and porches.

Two coats of paint for outside work. Varnish and wood filler for two coats of interior finish.

Built on a concrete block foundation, frame construction, sided with narrow bevel edge cypress siding and has cedar shingle roof. Notice the wood panel cornice, which is very becoming for this style of architecture.

All our houses that are of frame construction are sheathed with 1-inch boards and lined with the heaviest grade of building paper, and siding on the outside of the paper, thereby making very warm houses for the coldest climates.

Excavated basement under the entire house, 7 feet from floor to joists. First floor, 9 feet 2 inches from floor to ceiling; second floor 8 feet from floor to ceiling.

This house is 27 feet 6 inches wide by 40 feet 6 inches long and can be built on a lot 30 feet wide.

Complete Warm Air Heating Plant, for soft coal, extra	$ 85.76
Complete Warm Air Heating Plant, for hard coal, extra	87.81
Complete Steam Heating Plant, extra	153.65
Complete Hot Water Heating Plant, extra	196.09
Complete Plumbing Outfit, extra	109.60

SEARS, ROEBUCK AND CO.  CHICAGO, ILLINOIS

MODERN HOME No. 160

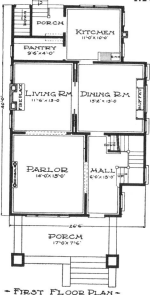

- FIRST FLOOR PLAN -

- SECOND FLOOR PLAN -

—53—

$1,163.00

For $1,163.00 we will furnish all the material to build this Seven-Room House, consisting of Mill Work, Ceiling, Flooring, Finishing Lumber, Building Paper, Pipe, Gutter, Sash Weights, Medicine Case, Buffet, Hardware, Mantel, Console, Painting Material, Lumber, Lath and Shingles. NO EXTRAS, as we guarantee enough material at the above price to build this house according to our plans.

By allowing a fair price for labor, cement, brick and plaster, which we do not furnish, this house can be built for about $2,695.00, including all material and labor.

For $48.00 extra we will furnish clear cypress bevel siding for the entire outside.

For Our Offer of Free Plans See Page 3.

A STRICTLY modern stonekote house with front porch 17x7 feet 6 inches, built-up columns and sided with stonekote to match the body of the house. Dublin front door glazed with bevel plate glass. Colored leaded Art Nouveau sash on each side of the center window on the second floor. Colored leaded art glass sash in stair hall, also over buffet in dining room.

Cased opening between the reception hall and parlor, also between parlor and living room. Double sliding doors between dining room and living room. Colonial buffet in the dining room. Mantel and fireplace in the living room. Console and large mirror in the parlor. Medicine case in bathroom. Oak open stairway in the hall with inside cellar stairs under the main stairs and outside cellar way in the rear. Inclosed rear porch.

Two-panel veneered oak interior doors and oak trim for first floor; five-cross panel yellow pine doors with soft pine stiles and rails and yellow pine trim for second floor. Oak flooring for main rooms first floor, with maple flooring for kitchen and pantry. Yellow pine flooring for the entire second floor and porches.

Varnish and wood filler for two coats of interior finish.

Built on a concrete foundation, frame construction, sided with stonekote, more commonly known as cement plaster, and has cedar shingle roof.

Excavated basement under the entire house, 7 feet from floor to joists, with cement floor. Rooms on the first floor are 9 feet from floor to ceiling; second floor, 8 feet 6 inches from floor to ceiling.

This house can be built on a lot 28 feet wide.

Complete Warm Air Heating Plant, for soft coal, extra	$ 90.73
Complete Warm Air Heating Plant, for hard coal, extra	92.74
Complete Steam Heating Plant, extra	193.64
Complete Hot Water Heating Plant, extra	238.07
Complete Plumbing Outfit, extra	118.80

SEARS, ROEBUCK AND CO.  CHICAGO, ILLINOIS

MODERN HOME No. 173

FIRST FLOOR PLAN

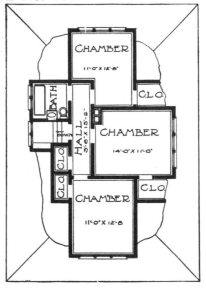

SECOND FLOOR PLAN

—54—

$924.00

For $924.00 we will furnish all the material to build this Six-Room House, consisting of Mill Work, Flooring, Ceiling, Finishing Lumber, Building Paper, Pipe, Gutter, Sash Weights, Hardware, Painting Material, Lumber, Lath and Shingles. NO EXTRAS, as we guarantee enough material at the above price to build this house according to our plans.

By allowing a fair price for cement, brick, plaster and labor, which we do not furnish, this house can be built for about $2,250.00, including all material and labor.

For Our Offer of Free Plans See Page 3.

A HIGH class six-room house with a large living room, 21 feet by 13 feet, opening to a large dining room with Roman colonnades between. A nice open staircase of oak in the front left hand corner of the living room, with a 5-foot stair landing which has four windows and a window seat on two sides.

The second floor contains three fair size bedrooms, four closets and bathroom.

The entire first floor trim, including front and inside doors, casings, base and open stairway, are of clear oak of modern Craftsman design. The entire second floor is trimmed with clear cypress casing, base, molding and cypress doors. Oak flooring in living room and dining room; yellow pine flooring for the kitchen, pantry, porch and entire second floor.

There is an entrance on the grade line, with a door under the main stairway which leads to the kitchen or to the basement.

This house is built on a concrete foundation and is of frame construction with stonekote finish, more commonly known as cement plaster, on the outside. Cedar shingle roof.

This house can be built on a lot 35 feet wide.

Complete Warm Air Heating Plant, for soft coal, extra.$	81.93
Complete Warm Air Heating Plant, for hard coal, extra	84.88
Complete Steam Heating Plant, extra	128.75
Complete Hot Water Heating Plant, extra	165.40
Complete Plumbing Outfit, extra	120.84

SEARS, ROEBUCK AND CO.  **CHICAGO, ILLINOIS**

MODERN HOME No. 181

FIRST FLOOR PLAN

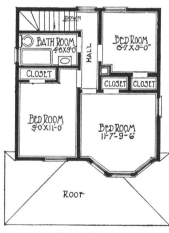

SECOND FLOOR PLAN

$687.00

For $687.00 we will furnish all the material to build this Six-Room House, consisting of Lumber, Lath, Shingles, Mill Work, Flooring, Ceiling, Siding, Finishing Lumber, Building Paper, Pipe, Gutter, Sash Weights, Hardware and Painting Material. NO EXTRAS, as we guarantee enough material at the above price to build this house according to our plans.

By allowing a fair price for labor, cement, brick and plaster, which we do not furnish, this house can be built for about $1,250.00, including all material and labor.

For Our Offer of Free Plans See Page 3.

A NEAT and roomy house at a very attractive price. Was designed with two objects in view, economy of floor space and low cost in construction. Contains six good rooms and bathroom. Porch is 22 feet by 8 feet. Front door opens into the living room which is 16 feet 1 inch long by 11 feet 6 inches wide. A door in the living room opens onto the closed stairway leading to the second floor. The dining room is separated from the living room by a large cased opening which makes practically one large room of these two rooms. Has kitchen and good size pantry. Entrance to the basement is through this pantry.

First Floor.

The front door is made of white pine, 1¾ inches thick. Inside doors are made of the best grade yellow pine and are of the five-cross panel design with yellow pine trim to match. Floors in living room and dining room are made of clear oak; the kitchen and pantry floors are maple. All floors on the first floor are laid over yellow pine floor lining.

Second Floor.

The stairway from the first floor opens into a hall on the second floor from which any one of the three bedrooms or bathroom may be entered. All three bedrooms are well lighted and each has a good size clothes closet.

All doors on the second floor are the best quality yellow pine of the four-panel design with yellow pine trim to match. Floors are of the best quality yellow pine.

Built on a concrete foundation and excavated under entire house. We furnish clear cypress siding and cedar shingles; framing timbers of the best quality yellow pine. All windows glazed with "A" quality glass.

Height of Ceilings.

Basement, 7 feet from floor to joist, with cement floor.
First floor, 9 feet from floor to ceiling.
Second floor, 8 feet 6 inches from floor to ceiling.
Painted with two coats of best paint outside, varnish and wood filler for interior finish.

This house can be built on a lot 28 feet wide.

Complete Warm Air Heating Plant, for soft coal, extra	$ 69.09
Complete Warm Air Heating Plant, for hard coal, extra	72.43
Complete Steam Heating Plant, extra	139.30
Complete Hot Water Heating Plant, extra	169.26
Complete Plumbing Outfit, extra	123.05

SEARS, ROEBUCK AND CO.  CHICAGO, ILLINOIS

$903.00

MODERN HOME No. 52

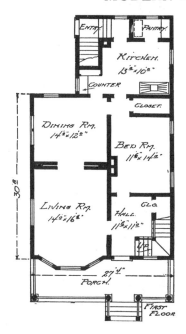

First Floor

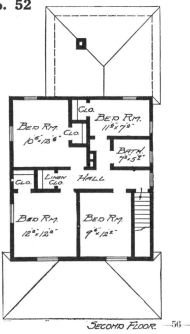

Second Floor

For $903.00 we will furnish all the material to build this Nine-Room House, consisting of Mill Work, Flooring, Ceiling, Finishing Lumber, Pipe, Gutter, Sash Weights, Hardware, Painting Material, Lumber, Lath and Shingles. NO EXTRAS, as we guarantee enough material at the above price to build this house according to our plans.

By allowing a fair price for labor, cement, brick and plaster, which we do not furnish, this house can be built for about $2,200.00, including all material and labor.

For Our Offer of Free Plans See Page 3.

A SQUARE concrete block residence with nine conveniently arranged rooms. Open stairway in the hall with closet underneath. Doors between stair hall and living room and between stair hall and bedroom. Double sliding doors between dining room and living room. Grade entrance opening to a landing with steps to the kitchen and also stairs to the cellar. Pantry in kitchen; closet in bedroom. On second floor are four bedrooms, four closets and bathroom.

Majestic front door, 1¾ inches thick, glazed with bevel plate glass. First floor inside doors, soft pine stiles and rails and five-cross yellow pine panels. Second floor doors, five-cross panels, clear soft pine. Clear yellow pine baseboard, casing and molding throughout the entire house. Yellow pine stairs of choice grain. Clear yellow pine flooring for first and second floors and porches.

Concrete block foundation made with 8x8x16-inch concrete blocks; cedar shingles for roof. Front porch, 27 feet 4 inches long by 9 feet wide; Colonial columns. Queen Anne attic and stair hall sash. Leaded Crystal front living room window.

Concrete block houses can be constructed at about one-third less than stone construction, and if properly built and well furred on the inside to make a dead air space between the blocks and the plaster, will be perfectly dry and healthful. A number of people apply the plaster directly to the block wall. We do not recommend this kind of construction unless you are sure that your concrete blocks are thoroughly waterproofed with a good waterproofing compound.

Excavated basement under the entire house, 7 feet 6 inches from floor to joists. Rooms on the first floor are 9 feet 4 inches from floor to ceiling; second floor, 8 feet 6 inches from floor to ceiling.

This house can be built on a lot 32 feet wide.

Complete Warm Air Heating Plant, for soft coal, extra	$ 93.59
Complete Warm Air Heating Plant, for hard coal, extra	95.66
Complete Steam Heating Plant, extra	175.80
Complete Hot Water Heating Plant, extra	224.00
Complete Plumbing Outfit, extra	137.00

SEARS, ROEBUCK AND CO.  **CHICAGO, ILLINOIS**

—56—

MODERN HOME No. 227

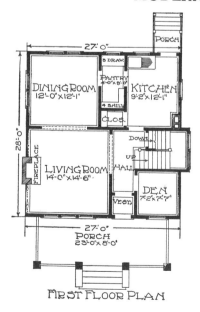

FIRST FLOOR PLAN

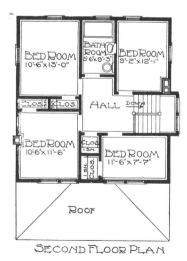

SECOND FLOOR PLAN

—57—

$934.00

For $934.00 we will furnish all the material to build this Seven-Room House, consisting of Lumber, Lath, Shingles, Mill Work, Ceiling, Siding, Flooring, Finishing Lumber, Building Paper, Pipe, Gutter, Sash Weights, Hardware, Mantel and Painting Material. NO EXTRAS, as we guarantee enough material at the above price to build this house according to our plans.

By allowing a fair price for labor, cement, brick and plaster, which we do not furnish, this house can be built for about $1,900.00, including all material and labor.

For Our Offer of Free Plans See Page 3.

A WELL designed house and one that will make a pleasant home. It is square in plan, giving the greatest amount of available space possible for the least money. The exterior presents a dignified and substantial appearance. Bevel siding is used for the first story, stonekote or cement for the second story. The large porch extending across the front is 23 feet wide by 8 feet deep. This house can be built with siding on the second story at about the same cost. The front door opens into a vestibule which separates the den from the hall. This vestibule could be dispensed with and the den would then be converted into a very nice reception hall. A large cased opening between the living room and dining room practically makes one large room of these two rooms. The pantry, which has plenty of shelving and a pantry case built in, is situated between the dining room and kitchen. This makes a very handy arrangement.

First Floor.

The front door is made of clear white pine, 1¾ inches thick, glazed with a long light of bevel plate glass. The vestibule door is also of clear white pine, glazed with "A" quality double strength glass. The inside doors are the five-cross panel design, made of the best quality yellow pine. Rear door, 1⅜ inches thick, made of soft pine and glazed with "A" quality double strength glass. Trim and flooring for the entire first floor are made of the best grade yellow pine.

Second Floor.

Stairway to second floor made of yellow pine, opens into a hall on the second floor, from which any of the four bedrooms, bathroom or linen closet may be entered. Three of the bedrooms have a good size clothes closet. All doors on the second floor are made of the best quality yellow pine in the five-cross panel style. Yellow pine trim and flooring.

Built on a concrete block foundation, excavated under the entire house. We furnish cypress siding and cedar shingles. Framing timbers of best quality yellow pine.

Height of Ceilings.

The basement has cement floor and is 7 feet from floor to joists. First floor is 9 feet from floor to ceiling; second floor, 8 feet 6 inches from floor to ceiling.

Painted two coats outside, varnish and wood filler for interior finish.

Should be built on a lot about 35 feet wide.

Complete Warm Air Heating Plant, for soft coal, extra	$ 92.14
Complete Warm Air Heating Plant, for hard coal, extra	94.15
Complete Hot Water Heating Plant, extra	215.44
Complete Steam Heating Plant, extra	180.45
Complete Plumbing Outfit, extra	120.06

SEARS, ROEBUCK AND CO.  **CHICAGO, ILLINOIS**

784^{00}

For $784.00 we will furnish all the material to build this Nine-Room House, consisting of Mill Work, Ceiling, Flooring, Finishing Lumber, Pipe, Gutter, Sash Weights, Hardware, Painting Material, Lumber, Lath and Shingles. NO EXTRAS, as we guarantee enough material at the above price to build this house according to our plans.

By allowing a fair price for labor, cement, brick and plaster, which we do not furnish, this house can be built for about $2,295.00, including all material and labor.

For Our Offer of Free Plans See Page 3.

A WELL PROPORTIONED and substantial city, suburban or country home with concrete porch 20 feet 6 inches by 7 feet. Concrete sides, steps and columns.

Oak open stairway in the reception hall. Cased opening between hall and parlor, and cased opening between dining room and parlor; door leading from the hall to the dining room. One bedroom and bathroom on the first floor. Closet in bedroom and one closet under the main stairs. Large china cupboard clear across one end of the kitchen, answering the purpose of a pantry. On the second floor are five bedrooms and four closets.

Beauty front door, 1¾ inches thick, veneered oak, glazed with bevel plate glass. Six-cross panel veneered oak inside doors for the first floor; clear oak trim with the exception of the cupboard. Oak floor for the first floor. Clear yellow pine doors, trim and flooring for the second floor.

Concrete block construction with rock face blocks up to the water table course and panel face blocks from the water table course to the second story window sill course. Plain face blocks the rest of the way up to cornice, and cedar shingle roof, with eaves curved at an 8-foot 9-inch radius, giving the roof a bell shape effect with 3-foot projection.

Our architects figured out the location and size of all doors and windows to come out just right by using full size and half size blocks, so that there will be no necessity of using any other size piece blocks. This makes the construction very easy and simple.

Excavated basement under the entire house, 7 feet 6 inches from floor to joists, with cement floor. Rooms on the first floor are 9 feet 5 inches from floor to ceiling; second floor, 8 feet 11 inches from floor to ceiling.

This house can be built on a lot 32 feet wide.

Complete Warm Air Heating Plant, for soft coal, extra	$ 97.29
Complete Warm Air Heating Plant, for hard coal, extra	99.30
Complete Hot Water Heating Plant, extra	228.13
Complete Steam Heating Plant, extra	178.50
Complete Plumbing Outfit, extra	117.44

SEARS, ROEBUCK AND CO.  **CHICAGO, ILLINOIS**

MODERN HOME No. 143

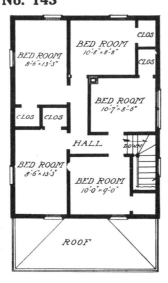

FIRST FLOOR PLAN

SECOND FLOOR PLAN

MODERN HOME No. 137

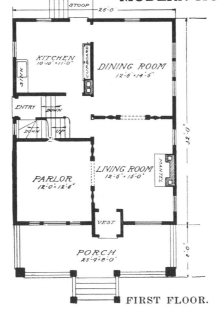

FIRST FLOOR.

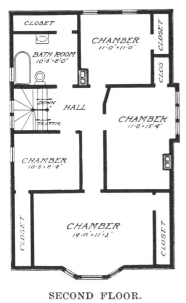

SECOND FLOOR.

—59—

$1,259⁰⁰

For $1,259.00 we will furnish all the material to build this Nine-Room House, consisting of Mill Work, Siding, Flooring, Ceiling, Finishing Lumber, Building Paper, Pipe, Gutter, Sash Weights, Hardware, Mantel, Painting Material, Lumber, Lath and Shingles. NO EXTRAS, as we guarantee enough material at the above price to build this house according to our plans.

By allowing a fair price for labor, cement, brick and plaster, which we do not furnish, this house can be built for about $2,750.00, including all material and labor.

For Our Offer of Free Plans See Page 3.

A COMBINATION siding and stonekote house with paneled gables; bay window in the front and side gables. Second story extends over the porch, forming the porch roof and making a great deal of room on the second floor. Queen Anne windows on the second floor with colored leaded art glass windows on the first floor, and front door also glazed with colored leaded art glass to match the windows.

Large living room with colonnade opening between the living room and parlor, and also colonnade between living room and dining room; mantel in living room. Open stairway and small hall connected with the living room, kitchen and dining room.

Ottawa front door. Two-panel veneered oak doors for the first floor; clear oak colonnades and stair trim. Five-panel yellow pine doors and yellow pine trim on the second floor. Oak floor for the first floor; clear yellow pine floor for the second floor and porches.

Built on a concrete block foundation, frame construction. First story sided with narrow bevel edge cypress siding; second story sided with stonekote and paneled with wood strips; cedar shingle roof.

Painted two coats outside; your choice of color. Varnish and wood filler for interior finish.

Excavated basement under the entire house, 7 feet 2 inches from floor to joists, with cement floor. Rooms on the first floor are 9 feet from floor to ceiling; second floor, 8 feet from floor to ceiling.

This house can be built on a lot 28 feet wide.

Complete Warm Air Heating Plant, for soft coal, extra	$ 89.88
Complete Warm Air Heating Plant, for hard coal, extra	94.03
Complete Steam Heating Plant, extra	152.95
Complete Hot Water Heating Plant, extra	201.52
Complete Plumbing Outfit, extra	133.00

SEARS, ROEBUCK AND CO.  **CHICAGO, ILLINOIS**

MODERN HOME No. 185

$637⁰⁰

For $637.00 we will furnish all the material to build this Seven-Room House, consisting of Lumber, Lath, Shingles, Mill Work, Flooring, Ceiling, Siding, Finishing Lumber, Building Paper, Pipe, Gutter, Sash Weights, Hardware and Painting Material. **NO EXTRAS**, as we guarantee enough material at the above price to build this house according to our plans.

By allowing a fair price for labor, cement, brick and plaster, which we do not furnish, this house can be built for about $1,250.00, including all material and labor.

For Our Offer of Free Plans See Page 3.

IN MODERN Home No. 185 we have a cottage of low cost, suitable for a 30-foot lot and is particularly adapted for a large family of moderate means. It will be seen from the floor plans that there is a large porch extending almost entirely across the front of the house. The front door opens into the living room. Either of the two bedrooms on the first floor or kitchen may be entered from the living room. A boxed stairway to the second floor has its entrance from the kitchen.

First Floor.

Front and rear doors are made of soft pine, 1⅜ inches thick, glazed with "A" quality double strength glass. Inside doors are of the five-cross panel style, and made of the best grade of yellow pine with yellow pine trim and flooring to match.

Second Floor.

The stairway opens into the small hall on the second floor, from which any of the three second floor bedrooms may be entered. Each bedroom on the second floor has a large closet. All doors on the second floor are made of the best grade of yellow pine, of the five-cross panel style. Floors and trim are also of yellow pine.

Built on a concrete block foundation. Not excavated. We furnish clear cypress siding and cedar shingles. Framing timbers are of the best quality yellow pine. "A" quality double strength glass used in all the windows. First floor height from floor to ceiling, 8 feet 6 inches. Second floor, 8 feet from floor to ceiling. Outside painted with two coats of the best paint. Varnish and wood filler for interior finish.

This house can be built on a lot 30 feet wide.

Complete Warm Air Heating Plant, for soft coal, extra............................	$ 65.58
Complete Warm Air Heating Plant, for hard coal, extra...........................	67.88
Complete Steam Heating Plant, extra..	127.50
Complete Hot Water Heating Plant, extra...	156.53

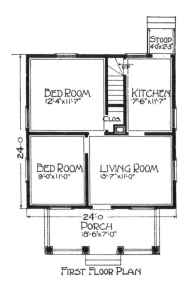

FIRST FLOOR PLAN

SECOND FLOOR PLAN

SEARS, ROEBUCK AND CO.  **CHICAGO, ILLINOIS**

MODERN HOME No. 121

$760⁰⁰

For $760.00 we will furnish all the material to build this Six-Room Cottage, consisting of Mill Work, Flooring, Siding, Ceiling, Finishing Lumber, Building Paper, Pipe, Gutter, Sash Weights, Mantel, Hardware, Painting Material, Lumber, Lath and Shingles. NO EXTRAS, as we guarantee enough material at the above price to build this house according to our plans.

By allowing a fair price for labor, cement, brick and plaster, which we do not furnish, this house can be built for about $1,602.00, including all material and labor.

For Our Offer of Free Plans See Page 3.

AN ATTRACTIVE six-room cottage for the family of moderate means. A good size front porch, 12 feet 3 inches by 7 feet, with a cluster of three Colonial columns on the outside corner and one column on each end next to the building. The front door enters directly into the dining room and there is a sliding door between the dining room and the parlor and a door from the dining room to the kitchen. Also a door connecting the parlor with the kitchen. Mantel and fireplace in the parlor. Closed stairway in the rear end of the dining room leading to the second floor. On the second floor are three good size chambers, bathroom and two closets.

Victoria front door glazed with leaded art glass. Five-cross panel inside doors; clear yellow pine trim throughout the house. Clear yellow pine flooring throughout the entire house and porches.

Painted two coats outside; your choice of color. Varnish and wood filler for interior finish.

Built on a concrete block foundation, frame construction, sided with narrow bevel edge cypress siding and has cedar shingle roof.

Excavated basement under the entire house, 7 feet from floor to joists. First floor, 8 feet 7 inches from floor to ceiling; second floor, 8 feet from floor to ceiling.

This house can be built on a lot 28 feet wide.

Complete Warm Air Heating Plant, for soft coal, extra	$ 78.67
Complete Warm Air Heating Plant, for hard coal, extra	81.10
Complete Steam Heating Plant, extra	133.66
Complete Hot Water Heating Plant, extra	169.97
Complete Plumbing Outfit, extra	118.22

SEARS, ROEBUCK AND CO.  **CHICAGO, ILLINOIS**

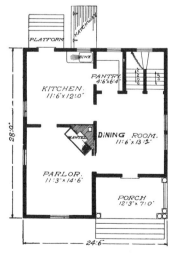

FIRST FLOOR PLAN.

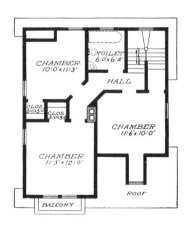

SECOND FLOOR PLAN.

MODERN HOME No. 144

$864.00

For $864.00 we will furnish all the material to build this Eight-Room Two-Story Bungalow, consisting of Mill Work, Ceiling, Siding, Flooring, Finishing Lumber, Building Paper, Pipe, Gutter, Sash Weights, Mantel, Hardware, Painting Material, Lumber, Lath and Shingles. NO EXTRAS, as we guarantee enough material at the above price to build this house according to our plans.

By allowing a fair price for labor, cement, brick and plaster, which we do not furnish, this bungalow can be built for about $2,035.00, including all material and labor.

For Our Offer of Free Plans See Page 3.

A MODERN style of eight-room bungalow of frame construction at a moderate price. The arrangement is ideal. Living room, dining room, library, kitchen and stair hall are located on the first floor; three bedrooms, trunk room and bathroom on second floor. The large porch with panel columns, 30 feet long by 8 feet wide, has balusters extending down to the grade line, producing a very pleasing effect.

First Floor.

The front vestibule leads directly into a wide hall which has cased openings with colonnades leading into a living room 11x14 feet and a dining room 11x12 feet, and also leading to stairway to second floor. Dining room has oak mantel, and plate rail around the entire room. The library, 8 feet 6 inches by 11 feet, is arranged directly in the rear of the living room, also with an entrance to back entry; can also be used as a bedroom. Kitchen, size 10 feet 4 inches by 11 feet. Directly off from the kitchen is the pantry with shelves and cupboards and door leading to rear entry. Inside stairway to basement from entry and also outside basement entrance.

Second Floor.

The stairs with landing leading to the second floor lead directly into a hall which connects with large bedroom 13x12 feet, with closet; also rear bedroom 11 feet by 14 feet 6 inches, with large trunk room or closet, size 7 feet 6 inches by 8 feet, adjoining, and chamber 8 feet 10 inches by 11 feet, with closet. Directly at the head of the stairs is the door leading to bathroom, size 11x9 feet. All rooms on both floors are light and airy.

For the front door we specify four-cross panel sash door, 1¾ inches thick, glazed with etched glass. Rear door of similar design with double strength glass. All interior doors on both first and second floors are five-cross panel design, made of clear yellow pine with casing, base and all molding to match. Floors on first and second floors of clear yellow pine; for porches edge grain yellow pine. Porch ceiled overhead with yellow pine beaded ceiling.

Built on concrete block foundation. Sided with narrow bevel siding on first floor; roof, dormer and second story covered with cedar shingles. All framing material, including joists, studding, etc., made from No. 1 yellow pine.

Excavated basement under entire house and with concrete floor.

Height of Ceilings: Basement, 6 feet 6 inches from floor to joists; first floor, 9 feet from floor to ceiling; second floor, 8 feet from floor to ceiling. Paint furnished for two coats and stain for siding shingles. Your choice of colors. Also varnish and wood filler for two coats of inside hard oil finish.

This house can be built on a lot 34 feet wide.

Complete Warm Air Heating Plant, for soft coal, extra	$ 76.04
Complete Warm Air Heating Plant, for hard coal, extra	79.30
Complete Steam Heating Plant, extra	162.65
Complete Hot Water Heating Plant, extra	193.30
Complete Plumbing Outfit, extra	108.10

SEARS, ROEBUCK AND CO.  CHICAGO, ILLINOIS

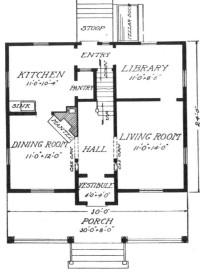

FIRST FLOOR PLAN

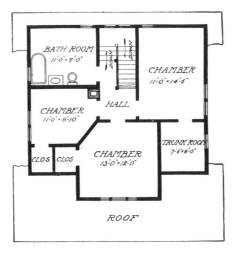

SECOND FLOOR PLAN

—62—

MODERN HOME No. 198

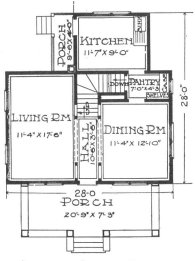

FIRST FLOOR PLAN

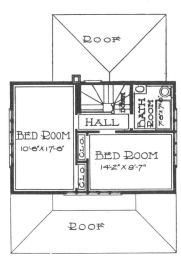

SECOND FLOOR PLAN

$834.00

For $834.00 we will furnish all the material to build this Five-Room Cottage, consisting of Lumber, Lath, Shingles, Mill Work, Ceiling, Siding, Flooring, Finishing Lumber, Building Paper, Pipe, Gutter, Sash Weights, Hardware and Painting Material. NO EXTRAS, as we guarantee enough material at the above price to build this house according to our plans.

By allowing a fair price for labor, cement, brick and plaster, which we do not furnish, this house can be built for about $1,700.00, including all material and labor.

For Our Offer of Free Plans See Page 3.

THIS attractive little home of five rooms and bath is well arranged. The exterior presents a neat and well balanced appearance and at the same time shows originality. It has a large porch, size 20 feet 9 inches wide by 7 feet 3 inches deep. The front door, which is of Craftsman design, opens into a hall which leads to the living room and the dining room and is separated from these two rooms by square columns and balustrades. The living room is 11 feet 4 inches wide by 17 feet 6 inches long with windows on two sides, admitting an abundance of light and air. The dining room is 11 feet 4 inches wide by 12 feet 10 inches long. The pantry, which is 7 feet long by 4 feet 3 inches wide, contains a pantry case and is situated between the dining room and kitchen, which makes a very convenient arrangement.

First Floor.

Front door is of veneered oak, 1¾ inches thick, made in Craftsman style. Also Craftsman design of panel door in dining room. The door leading to basement and kitchen is made of clear yellow pine, with five-cross panels. Rear door is of clear white pine, glazed with "A" quality double strength glass. Oak floor, and Craftsman style oak trim in the living room, hall and dining room. Clear yellow pine trim for kitchen and pantry.

Second Floor.

A beautiful oak stairway leads from first floor into a hall on the second floor, from which either of the bedrooms or bathroom may be entered. Both bedrooms are of good size and have large clothes closets. These clothes closets each have double doors; a very convenient arrangement.

Built on a concrete foundation. We furnish clear cypress siding and cedar shingles. Framing timbers are of the best quality yellow pine. Basement, 7 feet from floor to joists. First floor, 8 feet 6 inches from floor to ceiling; second floor, 8 feet 6 inches from floor to ceiling.

Painted with two coats of the best paint outside, varnish and wood filler for interior finish.

This house can be built on a lot 35 feet wide.

Complete Warm Air Heating Plant, for soft coal, extra	$ 66.64
Complete Warm Air Heating Plant, for hard coal, extra	69.90
Complete Steam Heating Plant, extra	142.85
Complete Hot Water Heating Plant, extra	179.71
Complete Plumbing Outfit, extra	120.19

SEARS, ROEBUCK AND CO.  **CHICAGO, ILLINOIS**

MODERN HOME No. 135

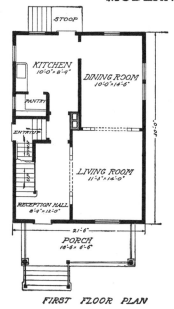

FIRST FLOOR PLAN

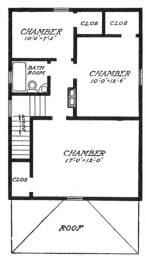

SECOND FLOOR PLAN

$791⁰⁰

For $791.00 we will furnish all the material to build this Seven-Room House, consisting of Mill Work, Siding, Flooring, Ceiling, Finishing Lumber, Building Paper, Pipe, Gutter, Sash Weights, Hardware, Painting Material, Lumber, Lath and Shingles. NO EXTRAS, as we guarantee enough material at the above price to build this house according to our plans.

By allowing a fair price for labor, cement, brick and plaster, which we do not furnish, this house can be built for about $1,620.00 including all material and labor.

For Our Offer of Free Plans See Page 3.

A VERY compact house with no space that cannot be used to the very best advantage. An extra large colonnade opening between the reception hall and living room, also between the living room and dining room, which practically throws these three rooms into one large room. In the reception hall there is an open stairway, the first tread having a circle end. Under the main stairs is an entrance on the grade line which leads to the kitchen or to the basement. When you land on the second floor at the head of the stairs you are within a very few feet from the entrance of all the bedrooms and bathroom on the second floor. Each room has a large closet.

Queen Anne front window for the front bedroom. Leaded Crystal window for the living room on the first floor. Windsor front door glazed with leaded glass to match the leaded window. All interior doors are five-cross panel, soft pine stiles and rails, yellow pine panels. Clear yellow pine casing, baseboard and molding throughout the entire house. Clear yellow pine flooring for the entire house and porches.

Painted two coats outside; your choice of color. Varnish and wood filler for interior finish.

Built on a concrete foundation, frame construction, sided with narrow bevel clear cypress siding, and has cedar shingle roof.

Excavated basement under the entire house, 7 feet from floor to joists. First floor, 9 feet from floor to ceiling; second floor, 8 feet 4 inches from floor to ceiling.

This house can be built on a lot 26 feet wide.

Complete Warm Air Heating Plant, for soft coal, extra.................$ 71.84
Complete Warm Air Heating Plant, for hard coal..................... 74.51
Complete Steam Heating Plant, extra................................ 139.15
Complete Hot Water Heating Plant, extra........................... 164.67
Complete Plumbing Outfit, extra................................... 98.50

SEARS, ROEBUCK AND CO.  **CHICAGO, ILLINOIS**

MODERN HOME No. 305

$1,238.00

For $1,238.00 we will furnish all the material to build this Ten-Room Two-Family Flat Building, consisting of Mill Work, Ceiling, Siding, Flooring, Finishing Lumber, Building Paper, Pipe, Gutter, Sash Weights, Hardware, Painting Material, Lumber, Lath and Shingles. NO EXTRAS, as we guarantee enough material at the above price to build this house according to our plans.

By allowing a fair price for labor, cement, brick and plaster, which we do not furnish, this house can be built for about $2,530.00, including all material and labor.

For Our Offer of Free Plans See Page 3.

A FLAT building arranged for one family on the first floor and one family on the second floor. Five rooms, bathroom, pantry and vestibule on the first floor. Five rooms, bathroom, pantry and alcove on the second floor. All rooms arranged to make use of every bit of space in the building. Large living rooms and kitchens. The rear bedroom in each flat can be very conveniently used for a dining room. The rear stairs built on the inside of the building enable the families in both flats to go to the basement or up to the attic without going outside.

Madison front door, 3x7 feet, 1¾ inches thick, glazed with lace design glass. All interior doors are five-cross panel clear yellow pine, and clear yellow pine trim, such as baseboard, casing, molding and stairs. Clear yellow pine flooring for porch floor and interior floors.

Built on a concrete block foundation, frame construction, and sided with narrow bevel clear cypress siding. Front gable has fancy window with a single sash on each side and is sided with stonekote, more commonly known as cement plaster. Cedar shingle roof. Front porch, 16 feet by 5 feet 6 inches, with Colonial columns.

Painted two coats outside; your choice of color. Varnish and wood filler for two coats of interior finish.

This house is built on very simple and plain lines of architecture and can be constructed at a very low cost and will prove a very good paying investment.

This house can be built on a lot 32 feet wide.

Complete Warm Air Heating Plant, for soft coal, extra	$119.25
Complete Warm Air Heating Plant, for hard coal, extra	124.04
Complete Steam Heating Plant, extra	224.53
Complete Hot Water Heating Plant, extra	262.52
Complete Plumbing Outfit, extra	190.00

SEARS, ROEBUCK AND CO.  CHICAGO, ILLINOIS

FIRST FLOOR PLAN.

SECOND FLOOR PLAN.

—65—

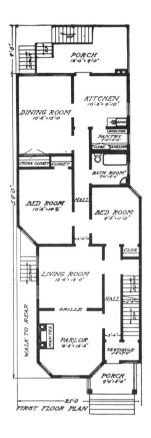

FIRST FLOOR PLAN

MODERN HOME No. 131

$1,727⁰⁰

For $1,727.00 we will furnish all the material to build this Thirteen-Room Two-Family Flat Building, consisting of Mill Work, Siding, Flooring, Ceiling, Finishing Lumber, Roofing, Building Paper, Pipe, Gutter, Sash Weights, Lumber, Lath, Hardware and Painting Material. NO EXTRAS, as we guarantee enough material at the above price to build this house according to our plans.

SECOND FLOOR PLAN

By allowing a fair price for labor, cement, brick and plaster, which we do not furnish, this house can be built for about $3,475.00, including all material and labor.

For Our Offer of Free Plans See Page 3.

THESE flats are conveniently arranged so that the parlor and living room with a large grille between practically make one large room with one bedroom on each side of the hall, having the windows on an angle, which assures that the light and ventilation will not be shut off in case other buildings are erected alongside. The dining room opens direct into the kitchen with two large windows on the rear, which makes a well lighted dining room. The bathrooms being directly over each other makes it possible for the same pipes to be used for the plumbing on the first and second floors, thereby making it possible to do the plumbing in the most economical manner. The parlor in each flat contains a mantel, and each dining room contains a china closet and a large pantry opening into the kitchen.

Beauty front door, veneered oak, glazed with bevel plate glass, is furnished for the front door. Interior doors for both flats are our Wilcox two-panel veneered birch of a very choice grain. The entire house is finished with clear birch casing, baseboard and moldings, with oak flooring in all rooms except kitchens, which is of maple.

This design of flat building is being put up in large numbers in many localities.

Built on a concrete block foundation and is of frame construction, sided with narrow bevel clear cypress siding and covered with 3½-Ply Best-of-all Roofing. Front porch, 9x6 feet, with Ionic columns and balcony overhead the same size as porch, and a large rear porch for each flat. Clear yellow pine flooring for porches.

The two front windows have a leaded colored art glass top of our Crescent design. All fair size windows, glazed with clear "A" quality double strength glass.

Painted two coats outside; your choice of color. Varnish and wood filler for two coats of interior finish.

Excavated basement under the entire building, 7 feet high from floor to joists, with a concrete floor. The rooms on the first floor are 9 feet from floor to ceiling; rooms on the second floor are 9 feet from floor to ceiling.

This flat building can be built on a lot 25 feet wide.

Complete Steam Heating Plant, extra..$233.95
Complete Hot Water Heating Plant, extra.......................................293.74
Complete Plumbing Outfit, extra..207.86

SEARS, ROEBUCK AND CO.  **CHICAGO, ILLINOIS**

—66—

$2,007⁰⁰

For $2,007.00 we will furnish all the material to build this Sixteen-Room Apartment Building, consisting of Mill Work, Flooring, Ceiling, Siding, Finishing Lumber, Building Paper, Roofing, Pipe, Gutter, Sash Weights, Hardware, Mantels, Painting Materials, Lumber and Lath. NO EXTRAS, as we guarantee enough material at the above price to build this house according to our plans.

By allowing a fair price for labor, cement, brick and plaster, which we do not furnish, this house can be built for about $4,510.00, including all material and labor.

For Our Offer of Free Plans See Page 3.

A FOUR-FAMILY apartment house with four rooms for each family, that can be built at a very low cost and will make an exceptionally good paying investment. The building of this house at a low cost is made possible by the economical arrangement of the plans, such as one single stairway to be used for both families on the second floor, and with but one front door and one vestibule. Having the two bathrooms on the first floor adjoining the same wall and the bathrooms on the second floor directly over the bathrooms on the first floor, thereby making it possible to use one set of plumbing pipes for all four bathrooms. One rear stair opening to each side to accommodate all the families in the building.

Each flat contains a mantel and fireplace in the living room. Two bedrooms, each with closet. One closet in the hall. Bathroom, nook, which is often used as an open closet, with a cased opening. Cupboard in the kitchen. A light court from the rear extending 18 feet 6 inches from the front to the rear, giving light and ventilation for the pantry, alcove, hall and bathrooms.

Majestic front door, 1¾ inches thick, glazed with bevel plate glass. Inside doors have soft pine stiles and rails with five-cross yellow pine panels. Clear yellow pine trim throughout the building. Clear yellow pine flooring throughout the building and porches.

Built on a concrete block foundation, frame construction, sided with narrow bevel clear cypress siding. Best-of-all Roofing. Front porch, 11 feet 9 inches by 6 feet. Colonial columns and newels. Colored leaded art Crescent window for the center window of each living room with Queen Anne side windows for each side of the triple windows.

Painted two coats outside; your choice of color. Varnish and wood filler for interior finish.

Excavated basement under the entire house, 7 feet 4 inches from floor to joists, with concrete floor and separated in two parts, each half being for two of the families in the building. Rooms on first floor, 9 feet from floor to ceiling; second floor, 9 feet from floor to ceiling. Skylight over stair hall.

This house can be built on a lot 36 feet wide.

Complete Warm Air Heating Plant, for soft coal, extra	$214.00
Complete Warm Air Heating Plant, for hard coal, extra	225.95
Complete Steam Heating Plant, extra	303.30
Complete Hot Water Heating Plant, extra	350.01
Complete Plumbing Outfit, extra	381.59

SEARS, ROEBUCK AND CO.  **CHICAGO, ILLINOIS**

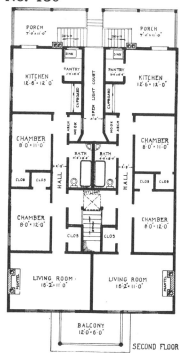

MODERN HOME No. 130

$836<u>00</u>

MODERN HOME No. 24

For $836.00 we will furnish all the material to build this Seven-Room House, consisting of Mill Work, Siding, Flooring, Ceiling, Finishing Lumber, Building Paper, Pipe, Gutter, Sash Weights, Hardware, Painting Material, Lumber, Lath and Shingles. NO EXTRAS, as we guarantee enough material at the above price to build this house according to our plans.

By allowing a fair price for labor, cement, brick and plaster, which we do not furnish, this house can be built for about $1,650.00, including all material and labor.

For Our Offer of Free Plans See Page 3.

THIS house makes a very comfortable country or suburban home, having large parlor, living room, kitchen and bedroom on the first floor, two large and one small bedroom on the second floor. While this house can be built for a very small cost, it is well arranged to accommodate a large family. The building of this house at this low cost is made possible by our furnishing you a high grade of material at low prices.

This house has our Garfield front door and the interior doors on the first floor are five-cross yellow pine panel doors. Doors on the second floor are four-panel clear yellow pine. All interior trim, such as baseboard, casing, molding, etc., is clear yellow pine, and yellow pine stairs. Clear yellow pine flooring for entire house and porches.

Built on concrete block foundation, frame construction, sided with narrow bevel edge cypress siding and has cedar shingle roof.

Painted two coats outside; your choice of color. Varnish and wood filler for interior finish.

Excavated basement under the entire house. Rooms on the first floor, 9 feet from floor to ceiling; rooms on the second floor, 8 feet 8 inches from floor to ceiling.

This house can be built on a lot 32 feet wide.

Complete Warm Air Heating Plant, for soft coal, extra	$ 77.01
Complete Warm Air Heating Plant, for hard coal, extra	79.06
Complete Steam Heating Plant, extra	176.72
Complete Hot Water Heating Plant, extra	230.42
Complete Plumbing Outfit, extra	112.54

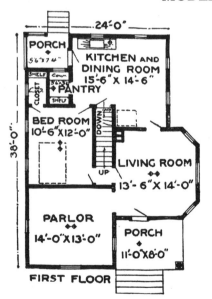

FIRST FLOOR

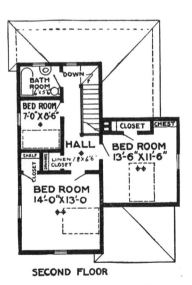

SECOND FLOOR

SEARS, ROEBUCK AND CO.  **CHICAGO, ILLINOIS**

$945⁰⁰

MODERN HOME No. 1232

For $945.00 we will furnish all the material to build this large Eight-Room House, consisting of Mill Work, Flooring, Ceiling, Siding, Finishing Lumber, Building Paper, Eaves Trough, Mantel, Hardware, Painting Material, Lumber, Lath and Shingles. NO EXTRAS, as we guarantee enough material at the above price to build this house according to our plans.

By allowing a fair price for labor, cement, brick and plaster, which we do not furnish, this house can be built for about $1,930.00, including all material and labor.

For Our Offer of Free Plans See Page 3.

EIGHT large and well arranged rooms, with vestibule and pantry on the first floor. Bathroom and three closets on the second floor. A great deal of room for a small amount of money. The parlor contains a mantel and fireplace and the living room has an open stairway which also is connected with the stairway from the kitchen, enabling one to go to the second floor from either of these two rooms. Cellar stairs directly under the main stairs with a door leading to it from both the kitchen and living room. Double sliding doors between living room and dining room.

Taylor front door. Nona pine five-cross panel interior doors on first floor. Doors on second floor are four-panel solid yellow pine. Interior yellow pine trim and yellow pine stair material, also yellow pine flooring for entire house and porches. Queen Anne windows on the second floor for the sides and front.

Built on a concrete block foundation, frame construction, sided with narrow bevel clear cypress siding and has cedar shingle roof.

Painted two coats outside; color to suit. Varnish and wood filler for two coats of interior finish.

Front porch, 10x14 feet; rear porch, 8 feet 4 inches by 7 feet 2 inches.

This house can be built on a lot 34 feet wide.

Complete Warm Air Heating Plant, for soft coal, extra	$ 84.02
Complete Warm Air Heating Plant, for hard coal, extra	86.03
Complete Steam Heating Plant, extra	197.35
Complete Hot Water Heating Plant, extra	236.37
Complete Plumbing Outfit, extra	111.45

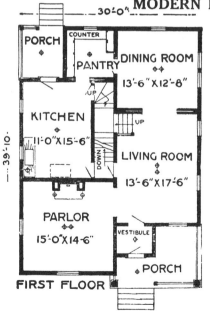

FIRST FLOOR

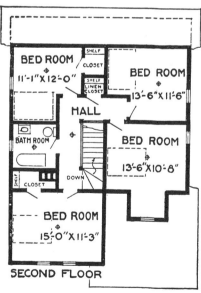

SECOND FLOOR

SEARS, ROEBUCK AND CO.  CHICAGO, ILLINOIS

—69—

$1,173.00

MODERN HOME No. 113

For $1,173.00 we will furnish all the material to build this Eight-Room House, consisting of Lumber, Lath, Shingles, Mill Work, Siding, Flooring, Ceiling, Finishing Lumber, Building Paper, Pipe, Gutter, Sash Weights, Hardware and Painting Material. NO EXTRAS, as we guarantee enough material at the above price to build this house according to our plans.

By allowing a fair price for labor, brick, cement and plaster, which we do not furnish, this house can be built for about $2,475.00, including all material and labor.

For Our Offer of Free Plans See Page 3.

A MODERN house with gambrel roof, large front porch, 22 feet by 6 feet 6 inches, and side porch 15x6 feet. The side entrance makes it very convenient for city or suburban residence or country home. The side porch could be very easily arranged to open up to a driveway which might be made directly at side of the house.

The rooms are very conveniently arranged with a large parlor or living room, 22 feet long by 13 feet wide, with a large reception hall, dining room and kitchen, and a nook in front of the reception hall. Three fair size bedrooms on the second floor and one large bedroom across the front, with a bay window, also bathroom, size 7 feet by 13 feet. Five large closets on the second floor; one closet on the first floor. Inside cellar entrance leading from the side entry with rear stairs to the second floor from the dining room; also an outside cellar entrance.

We furnish our Windsor front door glazed with leaded glass. All interior doors for the first and second floors are of clear solid yellow pine, five-cross panel. Our Crystal leaded glass window for the large window in the parlor, hall, bay window in the dining room and bay window in the front bedroom of the second floor. All interior trim, such as baseboard, casing and molding, is clear yellow pine. Clear yellow pine flooring for entire house and for porches. Built on a concrete block foundation, frame construction. Sided with clear cypress siding and roofed with cedar shingles.

Main open stairs are of unique pattern of clear plain sawed oak. Sufficient quantity of paint for two coats of exterior work. Varnish and wood filler for two coats of interior finish.

Excavated basement under the entire house, 7 feet 2 inches from floor to joists. Rooms on the first floor are 9 feet 2 inches from floor to ceiling; rooms on second floor, 8 feet from floor to ceiling.

This house is 27 feet 6 inches wide by 40 feet long and can be built on a lot 37 feet wide.

Complete Warm Air Heating Plant, for soft coal, extra	$ 92.33
Complete Warm Air Heating Plant, for hard coal, extra	94.41
Complete Steam Heating Plant, extra	178.58
Complete Hot Water Heating Plant, extra	239.45
Complete Plumbing Outfit, extra	135.10

SEARS, ROEBUCK AND CO.  **CHICAGO, ILLINOIS**

MODERN HOME No. 109

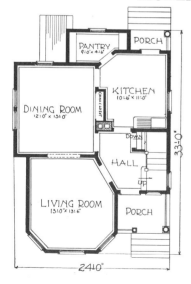

FIRST FLOOR PLAN

SECOND·FLOOR·PLAN

—71—

$676⁰⁰

For $676.00 we will furnish all the material to build this Seven-Room House, consisting of Mill Work, Siding, Flooring, Ceiling, Finishing Lumber, Building Paper, Pipe, Gutter, Sash Weights, China Closet, Hardware, Painting Material, Lumber, Lath and Shingles. NO EXTRAS, as we guarantee enough material at the above price to build this house according to our plans.

By allowing a fair price for labor, stone, brick and plaster, which we do not furnish, this house can be built for about $1,465.00, including all material and labor.

For Our Offer of Free Plans See Page 3.

A GOOD, substantial, well built house with all rooms of a fair size and arranged to make the best possible use of all the available space.
We furnish our Windsor front door glazed with leaded glass for the front with solid yellow pine five-cross panel doors for the interior for both first and second floors. Our Crystal leaded glass front window for the living room, with clear yellow pine trim, such as baseboard, casing, molding, etc., throughout the entire house, with open stairway with choice grain. Clear yellow pine flooring for entire house and porches.

Painted two coats outside; color to suit. Varnish and wood filler for two coats of interior finish.

This house is built on a stone foundation, 24 feet wide by 33 feet long, is of frame construction, sided with narrow bevel edge cypress siding and has cedar shingle roof.

Excavated basement under the entire house, 6 feet 8 inches from floor to joists. First floor, 9 feet 4 inches from floor to ceiling; second floor, 8 feet 4 inches from floor to ceiling.

This house can be built on a lot 27 feet 6 inches wide.

Complete Warm Air Heating Plant, for soft coal, extra	$ 68.87
Complete Warm Air Heating Plant, for hard coal, extra	71.96
Complete Steam Heating Plant, extra	170.63
Complete Hot Water Heating Plant, extra	201.52

SEARS, ROEBUCK AND CO.  **CHICAGO, ILLINOIS**

MODERN HOME No. 103

$726.00

For $726.00 we will furnish all the material to build this Six-Room House, consisting of Lumber, Lath, Shingles, Mill Work, Ceiling, Siding, Flooring, Finishing Lumber, Building Paper, Pipe, Gutter, Sash Weights, Hardware and Painting Material. NO EXTRAS, as we guarantee enough material at the above price to build this house according to our plans.

By allowing a fair price for labor, cement, brick and plaster, which we do not furnish, this house can be built for about $1,400.00, including all material and labor.

For Our Offer of Free Plans See Page 3.

A POPULAR design two-story house with side dormer. Houses of this design are being built in very large numbers in several localities as they afford a great deal of room for the amount of money invested. Notice the arrangement of the rooms in this house. An open stairway in the reception hall with cased opening between the reception hall and living room and cased opening between living room and dining room. Closet at the foot of the main stairs. Two large bedrooms on the second floor, four large closets and bathroom.

Artistic front door glazed with sand blast design glass. Five-cross panel, yellow pine interior doors, clear yellow pine trim for both first and second floors. Clear yellow pine flooring for entire house and porches.

Painted two coats outside; your choice of color. Varnish and wood filler for interior finish.

Built on a brick foundation, frame construction, sided with narrow bevel clear cypress siding and has cedar shingle roof. Colonial porch columns.

Excavated basement under the entire house, 6 feet 6 inches from floor to joists. First floor, 9 feet from floor to ceiling; second floor, 8 feet 6 inches from floor to ceiling.

This house measures 22x33 feet and can be built on a lot 25 feet wide.

Complete Warm Air Heating Plant, for soft coal, extra	$ 61.55
Complete Warm Air Heating Plant, for hard coal, extra	64.55
Complete Steam Heating Plant, extra	127.80
Complete Hot Water Heating Plant, extra	158.36
Complete Plumbing Outfit, extra	112.52

SEARS, ROEBUCK AND CO.  **CHICAGO, ILLINOIS**

FIRST FLOOR PLAN

THEY ARE ALL PLEASED WITH THE QUALITY.

Kenosha, Wis.

Sears, Roebuck and Co., Chicago, Ill.

Gentlemen:—On a lot of twenty-eight doors purchased from you I saved $16.00 after paying freight and drayage. Also saved 20 cents per window and received first class goods. Saved 40 per cent on eaves trough.
Yours truly,
O. E. CHANEY.

SECOND FLOOR PLAN

MODERN HOME No. 122

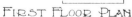

STOOD
10' 0" X 4' 0"

ENTRY
8' 6" X 4' 0"

SHELVES

PANTRY
8' 6" X 5' 0"

KITCHEN
12' 0" X 11' 0"

DOWN

UP

ENTRY

DINING ROOM
12' 0" X 14' 0"

RECEPTION
HALL
12' 0" X 9' 0"

VEST. CLO
4' 0" X 4' 6"

LIVING ROOM
13' 0" X 15' 0"

PORCH
8' 0" X 11' 0"

FIRST FLOOR PLAN

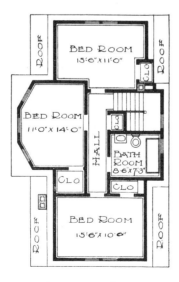

ROOF

BED ROOM
15' 6" X 11' 0"

CLO

BED ROOM
11' 0" X 14' 0"

HALL

CLO

BATH
ROOM
8' 6" X 7' 3"

CLO

CLO

BED ROOM
15' 6" X 10' 6"

ROOF

ROOF

ROOF

SECOND FLOOR PLAN

—73—

$1,057 00

For $1,057.00 we will furnish all the material to build this Seven-Room House, consisting of Lumber, Lath, Shingles, Mill Work, Siding, Flooring, Ceiling, Finishing Lumber, Building Paper, Pipe, Gutter, Sash Weights, Hardware, Mantel and Painting Material. NO EXTRAS, as we guarantee enough material at the above price to build this house according to our plans.

By allowing a fair price for labor, cement, brick and plaster, which we do not furnish, this house can be built for about $2,372.00, including all material and labor.

For Our Offer of Free Plans See Page 3.

A DESIGN that is popular in most all parts of the country, having a gambrel roof it is practical to build, as it can be built at a smaller cost than a full two-story house and yet contains practically the same amount of floor space.

The open birch stairway in the reception hall is a little out of the ordinary. Instead of the usual newel and rail it is paneled up 3 feet 6 inches high and finished with a wide ledge on top. Cased opening between the reception hall and dining room. Cased opening between the living room and dining room. Door between living room and reception hall and one door between the reception hall and kitchen. This enables you to go to any room on the first floor or to the second floor without passing through any of the other rooms. Mantel and fireplace in the living room and plate rail in the dining room. On the second floor are three large bedrooms and large bathroom, also four closets.

Queen Anne windows in the front of second floor with leaded Crystal cottage window in the living room. Hamilton birch front door glazed with leaded glass. First floor inside doors, two panel birch. Clear birch trim. Doors on the second floor are five-cross panel yellow pine with clear yellow pine moldings and trim. Oak flooring for the main rooms on the first floor; clear maple flooring for the kitchen and pantry; clear yellow pine flooring for second floor and porches.

Painted two coats outside; your choice of color. Varnish and wood filler for interior finish.

Concrete block foundation, frame construction, sided with narrow bevel edge clear cypress siding and has cedar shingle roof. Excavated basement under the entire house, 7 feet 4 inches from floor to joists. First floor, 8 feet 7 inches from floor to ceiling; second floor, 8 feet 6 inches from floor to ceiling.

This house can be built on a lot 28 feet wide.

Complete Warm Air Heating Plant, for soft coal, extra	$ 94.00
Complete Warm Air Heating Plant, for hard coal, extra	97.00
Complete Steam Heating Plant, extra	150.85
Complete Hot Water Heating Plant, extra	189.83
Complete Plumbing Outfit, extra	119.80

SEARS, ROEBUCK AND CO.

CHICAGO, ILLINOIS

MODERN HOME No. 241

$412.00

For $412.00 we will furnish all the material to build this Three-Room Bungalow, consisting of Lumber, Lath, Shingles, Mill Work, Flooring, Ceiling, Siding, Finishing Lumber, Building Paper, Pipe, Gutter, Sash Weights, Hardware and Painting Material. NO EXTRAS, as we guarantee enough material at the above price to build this house according to our plans.

By allowing a fair price for labor, cement, brick and plaster, which we do not furnish, this house can be built for about $900.00, including all material and labor.

For Our Offer of Free Plans See Page 3.

A TWENTIETH century bungalow. The popularity of cobblestones and boulders for foundations, pillars, chimneys and even for open fireplaces is unquestioned, and the effect obtained here through using cobblestones for a foundation and as porch pillars, in combination with shingles stained a rich brown as a siding, lends to its beauty.

The porch is 10 feet 4 inches wide by 5 feet 6 inches deep. The front door is made of clear white pine, 1¾ inches thick, and glazed with bevel plate glass. The combination living and dining room is 10 feet 4 inches wide by 19 feet long. The kitchen and bedroom are both of fair size, being each 9 feet wide by 10 feet 3 inches long. The bathroom is 7 feet 4 inches by 6 feet.

The interior doors are of the five-cross panel design, clear yellow pine, with yellow pine trim to match. The rear door is of soft pine, 1¾ inches thick, and glazed with clear glass. Yellow pine floors for entire house.

We furnish No. 1 yellow pine framing timbers. Cedar shingles for the roof and siding. Built on a cobblestone foundation, not excavated; 9 feet from floor to ceiling.

In order to have this house look its best, it should be built on a lot about 35 feet wide.

Complete Warm Air Heating Plant, for soft coal, extra............$47.89
Complete Warm Air Heating Plant, for hard coal, extra............ 51.20

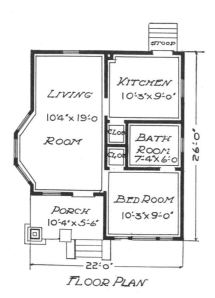

FLOOR PLAN

SEARS, ROEBUCK AND CO.  **CHICAGO, ILLINOIS**

MODERN HOME No. 159

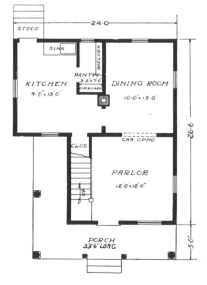

FIRST FLOOR PLAN

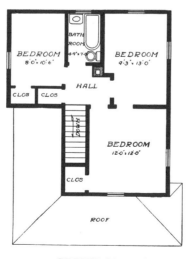

SECOND FLOOR PLAN

—75—

$652⁰⁰

For $652.00 we will furnish all the material to build this Six-Room Two-Story House, consisting of Lumber, Lath, Shingles, Mill Work, Ceiling, Siding, Flooring, Finishing Lumber, Building Paper, Pipe, Gutter, Sash Weights and Painting Material. NO EXTRAS, as we guarantee enough material to build this house according to our plans.

By allowing a fair price for labor, cement, brick and plaster, which we do not furnish, this house can be built for about $1,171.00, including all material and labor.

For Our Offer of Free Plans See Page 3.

THIS house is well arranged, having no waste space. Has six good size rooms, well lighted and ventilated with large windows. Is suitable for suburban or country home and has been frequently built in large numbers, proving to be a very good investment. It rents well, as it is practically two full stories high and of good appearance. It has a large front porch, 33 feet 6 inches long, with Colonial columns.

First Floor—Parlor with staircase leading to second floor. Cased openings from parlor to dining room. Has a large front window facing the street. Dining room and kitchen are of good size.

Second Floor—Has three good size bedrooms, three closets and bathroom.

At the above price we furnish a massive front door, 3x7 feet, 1¾ inches thick, glazed with bevel plate glass. Interior doors are five-cross panel with Nona pine stiles and rails and yellow pine panels. Clear yellow pine interior trim, such as baseboard, casing, molding and clear yellow pine staircase. Clear yellow pine flooring throughout house and porches.

This house is built on a concrete foundation, frame construction, sided with narrow bevel clear cypress siding and has cedar shingle roof.

Painted two coats outside; your choice of color. Varnish and wood filler for two coats of interior finish.

The rooms on the first floor are 9 feet from floor to ceiling; rooms on second floor, 8 feet from floor to ceiling.

This house can be built on a lot 27 feet wide.

Complete Warm Air Heating Plant, for soft coal, extra	$ 70.98
Complete Warm Air Heating Plant, for hard coal, extra	73.95
Complete Steam Heating Plant, extra	126.55
Complete Hot Water Heating Plant, extra	161.49
Complete Plumbing Outfit, extra	102.78

SEARS, ROEBUCK AND CO.  **CHICAGO, ILLINOIS**

MODERN HOME No. 108

FIRST·FLOOR·PLAN

SECOND·FLOOR·PLAN

—76—

$818.00

For $818.00 we will furnish all the material to build this Seven-Room House, consisting of Mill Work, Siding, Flooring, Ceiling, Finishing Lumber, Building Paper, Pipe, Gutter, Sash Weights, Hardware, Painting Material, Lumber, Lath and Shingles. NO EXTRAS, as we guarantee enough material at the above price to build this house according to our plans.

By allowing a fair price for labor, stone, brick and plaster, which we do not furnish, this house can be built for about $1,750.00, including all material and labor.

For Our Offer of Free Plans See Page 3.

A SPACIOUS house with seven large and well proportioned rooms. Open stairway in the reception hall. Cased opening between the reception hall and living room; also cased opening between living room and dining room, and there is access from the reception hall to the kitchen and dining room without passing through any of the other rooms. A large pantry. Inside cellar stairs directly under the main stairs, also an outside cellar stairway. Large bay window in the dining room. On the second floor are three bedrooms, large bathroom and four closets.

Victoria front door glazed with colored leaded art glass. Interior doors are five-cross panel yellow pine. Clear yellow pine trim on first and second floors; yellow pine flooring throughout the entire house and porches.

Built on a stone foundation, frame construction, sided with narrow bevel edge cypress siding and has cedar shingle roof.

Painted two coats outside; your choice of color. Varnish and wood filler for interior finish.

Excavated basement under the entire house, 7 feet from floor to joists, with cement floor. First floor, 9 feet from floor to ceiling; second floor, 8 feet 5 inches from floor to ceiling.

This house is 26 feet 6 inches wide by 35 feet 6 inches long and can be built on a lot 31 feet wide.

Complete Warm Air Heating Plant, for soft coal, extra	$ 81.00
Complete Warm Air Heating Plant, for hard coal, extra	83.48
Complete Steam Heating Plant, extra	150.25
Complete Hot Water Heating Plant, extra	191.74
Complete Plumbing Outfit, extra	112.39

SEARS, ROEBUCK AND CO.  **CHICAGO, ILLINOIS**

MODERN HOME NO. 240

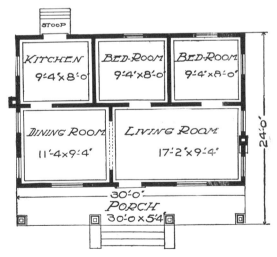

FLOOR PLAN

$422.00

For $422.00 we will furnish all the material to build this Five-Room Bungalow, consisting of Lumber, Lath, Shingles, Mill Work, Flooring, Ceiling, Siding, Finishing Lumber, Building Paper, Pipe, Gutter, Sash Weights, Hardware and Painting Material. NO EXTRAS, as we guarantee enough material at the above price to build this house according to our plans.

By allowing a fair price for labor, cement, stone and plaster, which we do not furnish, this house can be built for about $900.00, including all material and labor.

For Our Offer of Free Plans See Page 3.

A COTTAGE or bungalow sided with roughed 10-inch boards, laid 8 inches to the weather and stained with dark creosote stain. A cobblestone foundation, porch pillars and chimney give the bungalow a rustic beauty seldom seen in buildings at this low price. Front door opens into the living room, which is 17 feet 2 inches long by 9 feet 4 inches wide. Porch extends across the entire front. Size, 30 feet long by 5 feet 4 inches wide. Front door is made of clear white pine, 1¾ inches thick, glazed with bevel plate glass. Inside doors are five-cross panel style, clear yellow pine. Rear door is soft pine, 1¾ inches thick, and glazed with "A" quality double strength glass. The two cottage windows in the front are glazed with leaded crystal sheet glass in the top sash and "A" quality double strength glass in the bottom sash. All flooring and trim used in this house are made of the best grade yellow pine.

Built on a cobblestone foundation. Not excavated. We furnish framing timbers and siding of No. 1 yellow pine. Shingles are of cedar.

Height from floor to ceiling, 9 feet. Stain and paint are furnished for the exterior. Varnish and wood filler for the interior finish.

This lot on which this house is built should be at least 40 feet wide.

SEARS, ROEBUCK AND CO.  CHICAGO, ILLINOIS

MODERN HOME No. 110

$770⁰⁰

For $770.00 we will furnish all the material to build this Seven-Room House, consisting of Lumber, Lath, Shingles, Mill Work, Flooring, Ceiling, Siding, Finishing Lumber, Building Paper, Pipe, Gutter, Sash Weights and Painting Material. NO EXTRAS, as we guarantee enough material at the above price to build this house according to our plans.

By allowing a fair price for labor, stone, brick and plaster, which we do not furnish, this house can be built for about $1,615.00, including all material and labor.

For Our Offer of Free Plans See Page 3.

A COMFORTABLE home, suitable for a suburban or country residence. Has a large front porch, 25 feet long by 6 feet wide; Colonial porch columns. Rear porch, 11 feet by 4 feet 6 inches. Outside cellar entrance. Vestibule leads to the parlor and to the dining room. Cased opening between the dining room and parlor. Good size pantry and storeroom. Inside cellar stairs under the main stairs. Three bedrooms and two closets on the second floor, with an attic which is sometimes used as a storeroom or can be finished as a small bedroom, or it may be fitted up as a bathroom with little expense.

Windsor front door glazed with leaded glass. Inside doors are five-panel solid yellow pine; clear yellow pine molding and trim. Clear yellow pine flooring for the entire house and porches.

Painted two coats outside; your choice of color. Varnish and wood filler for interior finish.

Built on a stone foundation, frame construction, sided with narrow bevel edge cypress siding and has cedar shingle roof.

Excavated basement under the entire house, 6 feet 10 inches from floor to joists, with cement floor. First floor, 8 feet 6 inches from floor to ceiling; second floor, 8 feet from floor to ceiling.

This house is 24 feet 6 inches wide by 40 feet long and can be built on a lot 27 feet wide.

Complete Warm Air Heating Plant, for soft coal, extra	$ 67.68
Complete Warm Air Heating Plant, for hard coal, extra	70.59
Complete Hot Water Heating Plant, extra	175.62
Complete Steam Heating Plant, extra	141.92

SEARS, ROEBUCK AND CO.  **CHICAGO, ILLINOIS**

FIRST FLOOR PLAN

24'6"
40'0"

STORE RM
KITCHEN 9'6"X13'0"
PORCH
PANTRY
DINING ROOM 12'-0"X13'-0
BED ROOM 11'0"X10'0"
VESTIBULE 5'-6"X5'-6"
PARLOR 13'0"X12'0"
PORCH

SEEING OUR GOODS TELLS THE STORY OF QUALITY.

Pearl River, N. Y.

Sears, Roebuck and Co., Chicago, Ill.

Gentlemen:—I am very much pleased with the quality of the doors and trimmings, also the prompt delivery. The two-panel oak doors and the beamed ceiling are the talk of our neighborhood and have no doubt brought you many orders. Seeing is believing, and when prospective builders see the quality of the goods and the moderate price they have no hesitancy in ordering from you. The goods you sent me are the best advertisement you could have in our section.

Very truly yours,

FRANK GARDINER.

ATTIC (FLOORED)
ROOF
ROOF
BED ROOM 9'-6"X10'0"
HALL
BED ROOM 10'-0"X 7'-0"
CLOSET
CLOS.
BED ROOM 13'-0"X12'0"
ROOF
ROOF

SECOND FLOOR PLAN

MODERN HOME No. 101

$841.00

For $841.00 we will furnish all the material to build this Eight-Room House, consisting of Lumber, Lath, Shingles, Mill Work, Ceiling, Siding, Flooring, Finishing Lumber, Building Paper, Pipe, Gutter, Sash Weights, Hardware and Painting Material. NO EXTRAS, as we guarantee enough material at the above price to build this house according to our plans.

By allowing a fair price for labor, stone, brick and plaster, which we do not furnish, this house can be built for about $1,875.00, including all material and labor.

For Our Offer of Free Plans See Page 3.

ROOMS are large and well proportioned. Front door enters directly into the living room. Sliding door between the living room and parlor, and sliding door between living room and library. Large kitchen, pantry, bathroom or storeroom on the first floor. Inside cellar stairs directly under the main stairs, and outside cellar entrance in the rear. On the second floor is one large front chamber with two medium size side bedrooms, three closets and large storeroom over kitchen which can be used as a bedroom.

Rich front door glazed with leaded art glass; clear yellow pine interior doors for both first and second floors. Yellow pine casing, baseboard and trim. Leaded Crystal front window for parlor. Yellow pine flooring for the entire house and porches.

Built on a stone foundation, frame construction, sided with narrow bevel cypress siding and cedar shingle roof.

Painted two coats outside; your choice of color. Varnish and wood filler for interior finish.

Excavated basement under the entire house, 6 feet 10 inches from floor to joists. First floor, 9 feet 2 inches from floor to ceiling; second floor, 8 feet 6 inches from floor to ceiling.

This house measures 26x44 feet and can be built on a lot 30 feet wide.

Complete Warm Air Heating Plant, for soft coal, extra	$ 74.79
Complete Warm Air Heating Plant, for hard coal, extra	76.36
Complete Steam Heating Plant, extra	177.85
Complete Hot Water Heating Plant, extra	199.16

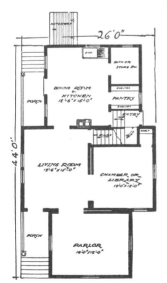

— FIRST FLOOR PLAN —

— SECOND FLOOR PLAN —

SEARS, ROEBUCK AND CO.  **CHICAGO, ILLINOIS**

MODERN HOME No. 199

FIRST FLOOR PLAN

SECOND FLOOR PLAN

$558.00

For $558.00 we will furnish all the material to build this Five-Room Cottage, consisting of Lumber, Lath, Shingles, Mill Work, Flooring, Ceiling, Siding, Finishing Lumber, Building Paper, Pipe, Gutter, Sash Weights, Hardware and Painting Material. NO EXTRAS, as we guarantee enough material at the above price to build this house according to our plans.

By allowing a fair price for labor, cement, brick and plaster, which we do not furnish, this house can be built for about $1,100.00, including all material and labor.

For Our Offer of Free Plans See Page 3.

A NICELY arranged home of five rooms and bath. This cottage can be built at a low cost and will go nicely on a 25-foot lot. Front door opens into the living room which is 14 feet long by 11 feet wide. A large cased opening between the living room and dining room practically makes one large room of these two rooms. The kitchen is just a nice size, being 8 feet 7 inches wide by 9 feet 6 inches long. Has a good size pantry with pantry case built in. The cellar stairs have their entrance in the kitchen and are immediately under the stairs leading from the first floor to the second floor.

First Floor.

Front door is made of soft pine, 1⅜ inches thick, glazed with "A" quality double strength glass. All inside doors are made of yellow pine and are of the four-panel style, with best quality yellow pine trim and floors. Rear door is of soft pine 1⅜ inches thick and glazed with "A" quality double strength glass.

Second Floor.

The stairs open into the hall on the second floor, from which any of the bedrooms or the bathroom may be entered. Each of the bedrooms has a clothes closet. Bathroom is 6 feet 6 inches wide by 8 feet 2 inches long. All doors are of the four-panel style, made of the best quality of yellow pine. Yellow pine trim and floors.

Built on a concrete foundation. Excavated under the entire house. We furnish clear cypress siding and cedar shingles. Framing timbers are of the best quality yellow pine. Basement is 7 feet from floor to joists. First floor, 8 feet 6 inches from floor to ceiling; second floor, 8 feet from floor to ceiling.

Painted two coats of best paint outside, varnish and wood filler for interior finish.

This house can be built on a lot 25 feet wide.

Complete Warm Air Heating Plant, for soft coal, extra	$62.04
Complete Warm Air Heating Plant, for hard coal, extra	65.34
Complete Steam Heating Plant, extra	101.00
Complete Hot Water Heating Plant, extra	128.07
Complete Plumbing Outfit, extra	119.71

SEARS, ROEBUCK AND CO.  **CHICAGO ILLINOIS**

$917⁰⁰

For $917.00 we will furnish all the material to build this Eight-Room House, consisting of Mill Work, Siding, Flooring, Ceiling, Finishing Lumber, Building Paper, Pipe, Gutter, Sash Weights, Hardware, Painting Material, Lumber, Lath and Shingles. NO EXTRAS, as we guarantee enough material at the above price to build this house according to our plans.

By allowing a fair price for labor, cement, brick and plaster, which we do not furnish, this house can be built for about $1,900.00, including all material and labor.

For Our Offer of Free Plans See Page 3.

A GOOD, substantial house, suitable for town, suburban or country home. All rooms are of good size and well arranged for convenience. China closet built into the wall of the dining room. Large cased opening between the sitting room and dining room, which practically makes these two rooms into one large room. Has an open stairway in the sitting room which faces directly toward the entrance of the parlor. Inside cellar way leading to the basement from the hall. Bathroom on the first floor. Three large bedrooms on the second floor, all of which could be used with two beds if necessary.

Blaine front door, leaded Crystal front window. Interior doors on first floor have Nona pine stiles and rails with five-cross yellow pine panels. Second floor doors are our special high grade painted four-panel doors. Clear yellow pine trim for both first and second floors and yellow pine open stairs. Yellow pine flooring for entire house and porches.

Built on a concrete block foundation, frame construction, sided with narrow bevel edge cypress siding and has cedar shingle roof.

Painted two coats outside; color to suit. Varnish and wood filler for two coats of interior finish.

Excavated basement under the entire house, 6 feet 3 inches high. First floor, 9 feet from floor to ceiling; second floor, 8 feet from floor to ceiling. Outside measurement, 27 feet 6 inches by 47 feet.

This house is 27 feet 6 inches wide by 47 feet long and can be built on a lot 30 feet wide.

Complete Warm Air Heating Plant, for soft coal, extra	$ 91.13
Complete Warm Air Heating Plant, for hard coal, extra	93.10
Complete Steam Heating Plant, extra	177.75
Complete Hot Water Heating Plant, extra	227.23
Complete Plumbing Outfit, extra	100.59

SEARS, ROEBUCK AND CO.  **CHICAGO, ILLINOIS**

MODERN HOME No. 116

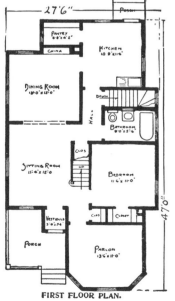

FIRST FLOOR PLAN.

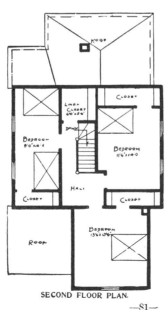

SECOND FLOOR PLAN.

—81—

MODERN HOME No. 105

$531⁰⁰

For $531.00 we will furnish all the material to build this Five-Room House, consisting of Mill Work, Siding, Flooring, Ceiling, Finishing Lumber, Building Paper, Pipe, Gutter, Sash Weights, Hardware, Painting Material, Lumber, Lath and Shingles. NO EXTRAS, as we guarantee enough material at the above price to build this house according to our plans.

By allowing a fair price for labor, stone, brick and plaster, which we do not furnish, this house can be built for about $1,190.00, including all material and labor.

For Our Offer of Free Plans See Page 3.

A TWO-STORY HOUSE having three rooms on the first floor with pantry and closet. Inside cellar stairway under the main stairs. Outside cellar entrance in the rear. Two rooms on the second floor and closet in each room, with two windows in each room, making them well lighted and perfectly ventilated. Front porch is 20x5 feet, with Colonial columns.

Our Cass front door. Yellow pine inside doors and trim. Clear yellow pine flooring throughout the entire house and porches.

Painted two coats outside; your choice of color. Varnish and wood filler for interior finish.

Built on a stone foundation, frame construction, sided with narrow bevel edge cypress siding and has a cedar shingle roof.

This house is 22 feet wide by 27 feet 6 inches long and can be built on a lot 25 feet wide.

Complete Warm Air Heating Plant, for soft coal, extra	$ 54.98
Complete Warm Air Heating Plant, for hard coal, extra	58.22
Complete Steam Heating Plant, extra	101.10
Complete Hot Water Heating Plant, extra	123.62
Complete Plumbing Outfit, extra	103.63

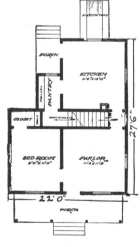

— FIRST FLOOR PLAN —

—82—

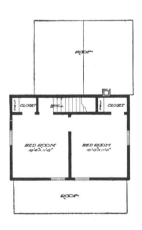

— SECOND FLOOR PLAN —

SEARS, ROEBUCK AND CO.  **CHICAGO, ILLINOIS**

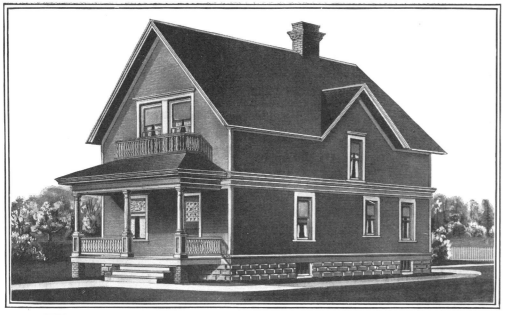

MODERN HOME No. 117

FIRST FLOOR.

PORCH	7'×11'6"
KITCHEN	16'×11'
PANTRY	9'×8'
DINING ROOM	13'6"×13'
SITTING ROOM	9'0"×15'
PARLOR	13'6"×14'
VES	
PORCH	19'×5'

SECOND FLOOR

BED ROOM	23'×11
BED ROOM	12'×13
BED ROOM	23'×14
ROOF	

WE PACK OUR MATERIAL SO THAT IT REACHES OUR CUSTOMERS IN GOOD CONDITION AND SAVE THEM 25 TO 50 PER CENT.

Lyons, Ga.

Sears, Roebuck and Co., Chicago, Ill.

Gentlemen:—Building material and mill work bought of you recently have all been received and put up. All came in first class order, so well packed that not a glass was broken. Doors, sash and blinds far superior in quality at the price to material of same kind in this market, Savannah, Ga., included. We saved from 25 to 50 per cent by ordering from you. We thank you for same. Whenever we need any goods in the future for building purposes will be sure to give you our order. We are now in our new home, well fixed, etc.

Yours respectfully,

MRS. CARRIE E. BRASWELL.

$848.00

For $848.00 we will furnish all the material to build this Seven-Room House, consisting of Mill Work, Lumber, Lath, Shingles, Flooring, Ceiling, Siding, Finishing Lumber, Eaves Trough, Hardware and Painting Material. NO EXTRAS, as we guarantee enough material at the above price to build this house according to our plans.

By allowing a fair price for labor, cement, brick and plaster, which we do not furnish, this house can be built for about $2,000.00, including all material and labor.

For Our Offer of Free Plans See Page 3.

THIS house is handily arranged, all rooms being of good size and so planned that there is hardly a foot of waste space. A large cased opening between the dining room and parlor makes these two rooms practically into one large room which is frequently used as a parlor and back parlor, and the kitchen being so large is often used as a kitchen and dining room, and the sitting room as a bedroom for the first floor. You will note the two large bedrooms on the second floor, each one extending clear across the house, one on the front and the other on the rear.

The front door is our Victoria design, glazed with colored leaded art glass. The inside doors are five-panel solid clear yellow pine for both first and second floors. All the interior trim, such as baseboard, casing, molding and stairs, is clear yellow pine. Front parlor window is our Crescent design, glazed colored leaded art glass. Clear yellow pine flooring for entire house and porches.

Painted two coats outside; your choice of color. Varnish and wood filler for interior finish.

This house is built on a concrete block foundation and is of frame construction, sided with narrow bevel clear cypress siding and has cedar shingle roof.

Excavated basement under the entire house, 7 feet from floor to joists. First floor, 9 feet 4 inches from floor to ceiling; second floor, 8 feet from floor to ceiling.

This house can be built on a lot 27 feet wide.

Complete Warm Air Heating Plant, for soft coal, extra...............$ 88.79
Complete Warm Air Heating Plant, for hard coal, extra............... 90.80
Complete Steam Heating Plant, extra................................. 150.15
Complete Hot Water Heating Plant, extra............................ 193.05

SEARS, ROEBUCK AND CO.  **CHICAGO, ILLINOIS**

$1,019.00

MODERN HOME No. 34

For $1,019.00 we will furnish all the material to build this Eight-Room House, consisting of Mill Work, Flooring, Ceiling, Finishing Lumber, Building Paper, Pipe, Gutter, Sash Weights, Hardware, Painting Material, Lumber, Lath and Shingles. NO EXTRAS, as we guarantee enough material at the above price to build this house according to our plans.

By allowing a fair price for labor, cement, brick and plaster, which we do not furnish, this house can be built for about $1,970.00, including all material and labor.

For Our Offer of Free Plans See Page 3.

A GOOD, well built, roomy house. Large parlor connects with the dining room by large cased opening. Good size kitchen and bedroom on the first floor. Reception hall connects with the parlor by sliding door and contains an open stairway of choice grain clear yellow pine.

Front door glazed with lace design glass. Interior doors for main rooms on first floor are five-cross panel with soft pine stiles and rails and yellow pine panels. Doors on the second floor are four-panel solid yellow pine. Clear yellow pine interior trim throughout the house. Our Crystal leaded glass sash for side bay window and front window in the parlor, with leaded glass sash in the stair hall to match. Three Queen Anne windows in the front bedroom of the second floor. Clear yellow pine flooring for the entire house and porches.

Built on a concrete block foundation, frame construction, sided with narrow bevel clear cypress siding and has cedar shingle roof. Colonial porch columns.

Painted two coats outside; color to suit. Varnish and wood filler for two coats of interior finish.

Excavated basement under the entire house, 7 feet from floor to joists. First floor, 9 feet from floor to ceiling; second floor, 8 feet 6 inches from floor to ceiling.

This house can be built on a lot 32 feet wide.

Complete Warm Air Heating Plant, for soft coal, extra	$ 84.89
Complete Warm Air Heating Plant, for hard coal, extra	86.92
Complete Steam Heating Plant, extra	177.22
Complete Hot Water Heating Plant, extra	198.52

SEARS, ROEBUCK AND CO.  **CHICAGO, ILLINOIS**

FIRST FLOOR PLAN

WOOD ROOM
KITCHEN 12'-6"X12'-0"
PANTRY
DINING ROOM 14'-0"X17'-6"
BED ROOM 13'-0"X14'-0"
ARCH
CLOSET
PARLOR 15'-0"X15'-0"
HALL
26'-0"
PORCH 26'-0"X10'-0"
43'-0"

HAS BUILT THREE OF OUR MODERN HOMES AND IS NOW BUILD-ING THE FOURTH.

Hillsdale, Mich.
Sears, Roebuck and Co., Chicago, Ill.

Gentlemen:—I have built one house No. 111 Modern Home; made a few changes, but I will say that the plans are complete. I have built two houses after Modern Home No. 34 and am now starting the third. I am a contractor and builder. I have bought lots of mill work of you people and have always been satisfied. I now have an order and expect to send another this week. By buying your material, Modern Home No. 111 can be built in Hillsdale, Mich., for $1,950.00; Modern Home No. 34 can be built for $1,600.00. Your blue prints are the finest I have ever seen. I have built two houses from plans bought from another well known firm for $30.00 and the prints are not worth one-fourth as much as yours.
S. E. FULLER.

ROOF
BED ROOM 14'-0"X14'-0"
BED ROOM 13'-0"X14'-0"
CLOSET
CLOSET
HALL
DOWN
CLOSET
BED ROOM 17'-0"X11'-0"
ROOF

SECOND FLOOR PLAN

MODERN HOME No. 171

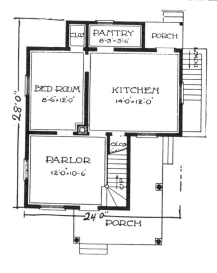

FIRST FLOOR

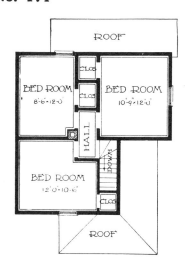

SECOND FLOOR

—85—

$544.00

For $544.00 we will furnish all the material to build this Six-Room Cottage, consisting of Mill Work, Flooring, Ceiling, Siding, Finishing Lumber, Building Paper, Pipe, Gutter, Sash Weights, Hardware, Painting Material, Lumber, Lath and Shingles. NO EXTRAS, as we guarantee enough material at the above price to build this house according to our plans.

By allowing a fair price for labor, cement, brick and plaster, which we do not furnish, this house can be built for about $950.00, including all material and labor.

For Our Offer of Free Plans See Page 3.

IN MODERN Home No. 171 we have a very neat appearing and up to date cottage at a very low cost. By reason of its simple outline and the entire absence of complicated details, the labor is but a small item of expense as compared with the average house of this size.

On the first floor there are three fair size rooms and pantry. Open stairway leading from the parlor to the second floor. The first and second floors are finished in yellow pine; doors have soft pine stiles and rails and yellow pine panels. In the parlor is a large cottage window; front door glazed with lace design glass. Three large size bedrooms, each having a closet. The flooring for both the first and second floors and porches is of No. 1 yellow pine. This cottage is so arranged that the ventilation is perfect throughout the house, and yet so compact that it may be heated at a very low cost.

There is an excavated basement under the kitchen, 7 feet from floor to joists. This cottage is built on a concrete block foundation. Frame construction, sided with narrow bevel clear cypress siding and has cedar shingle roof.

This house can be built on a lot 26 feet wide.

Complete Warm Air Heating Plant, for soft coal, extra........................... $66.97
Complete Warm Air Heating Plant, for hard coal, extra........................... 69.88

SEARS, ROEBUCK AND CO.  CHICAGO, ILLINOIS

$539.00

For $539.00 we will furnish all the material to build this cozy Six-Room Story and a Half House with frame construction, consisting of Lumber, Lath, Shingles, Mill Work, Building Paper, Eaves Trough, Hardware and Painting Material. NO EXTRAS, as we guarantee enough material at the above price to build this house according to our plans.

By allowing a fair price for labor, cement, brick and plaster, which we do not furnish, this house can be built for about $870.00, including all material and labor.

For Our Offer of Free Plans See Page 3.

A WELL and economically arranged six-room story and a half house, built of the same good material as specified in even our higher priced houses shown in this book. Over fifty houses of this design were built during the past year and every one of them has satisfied the owner in price, quality and the big saving we made them. Most of the houses were built at a lower price than we estimated.

A porch, 5 feet in width, extends across the front 11 feet, and 11 feet along the side, giving ample porch room.

First Floor.

Front door leads to the parlor and to enclosed stairway leading to the second floor. Directly in the rear of the parlor is located a good size bedroom with closet, with doors leading from bedroom to parlor and from bedroom to kitchen. Kitchen measures 14 feet by 11 feet 9 inches, giving ample room for kitchen and dining room combined. Directly off kitchen is a large pantry with shelves and a door leading to rear porch.

This house has an attractive white pine paneled front door with ornamental lace design glass. Rear outside door five-cross panel No. 1 yellow pine. Interior doors No. 1 quality four-panel yellow pine, all of which are 1⅜ inches thick. All casing, baseboards, molding and staircase are made of clear yellow pine. Yellow pine flooring throughout.

Second Floor.

On the second floor is located two medium size bedrooms with closets, all lathed and plastered, and one large room unfinished which can be used as a storage room or converted into a very large bedroom at little additional expense for lath and plaster. All doors, casing, baseboard, moldings and floors are of clear yellow pine and intended for oil finish.

Built on well constructed wood foundation and of frame construction. Covered with clear narrow bevel cypress siding and roof covered with *A* cedar shingles.

Paint furnished for two coats for exterior work, your choice of colors. Sufficient wood filler and varnish furnished for two coats of interior finish.

A saving of about $25.00 can be made by using our 3½-ply Best-of-all Roofing instead of cedar shingles; same guaranteed to last equally as long as the best quality of cedar shingles.

Excavated cellar, 7 feet 6 inches wide by 11 feet 6 inches long, 7 feet from floor to joists. First floor, 8 feet 6 inches from floor to ceiling.

Second floor, 8 feet from floor to ceiling.

This house can be built on a lot 26 feet wide.

Complete Warm Air Heating Plant, for soft coal, extra	$ 53.85
Complete Warm Air Heating Plant, for hard coal, extra	57.17
Complete Steam Heating Plant, extra	95.13
Complete Hot Water Heating Plant, extra	113.92

SEARS, ROEBUCK AND CO. — QUALITY GUARANTEED — **CHICAGO, ILLINOIS**

MODERN HOME No. 115

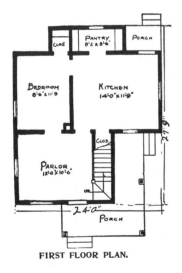

FIRST FLOOR PLAN.

SECOND FLOOR PLAN.

MODERN HOME No. 141

FLOOR PLAN

821 Foster Ave., Cambridge, Ohio.

Sears, Roebuck and Co., Chicago, Ill.

Gentlemen:—I received nineteen doors, two stair newels, one stair rail and eight corner blocks. I saved $15.00 on this order. I have been working at the carpenter trade for ten years and never put up better doors. I help to build from ten to fifteen houses a year. They run in price from $1,500.00 to $4,000.00. I am well pleased with this order.

Very truly yours,

C. W. VALENTINE.

$476.00

For $476.00 we will furnish all the material to build this Four-Room Cottage, consisting of Mill Work, Flooring, Siding, Ceiling, Finishing Lumber, Building Paper, Pipe, Gutter, Sash Weights, Hardware, Painting Material, Lumber, Lath and Shingles. NO EXTRAS, as we guarantee enough material at the above price to build this house according to our plans.

By allowing a fair price for labor, brick and plaster, which we do not furnish, this house can be built for about $850.00, including all material and labor.

For Our Offer of Free Plans See Page 3.

A FOUR-ROOM COTTAGE with large pantry and two closets. Good size front porch, 16 feet by 6 feet. Large attic which could well be finished into two rooms if desired.

Metropole front door glazed with sand blast design glass. Clear yellow pine inside molding and trim. Clear yellow pine flooring for the house and porches.

Painted two coats outside; your choice of color. Varnish and wood filler for interior finish.

Built on a frame foundation. Frame construction, sided with narrow bevel clear cypress siding and has cedar shingle roof. Rooms are 9 feet from floor to ceiling.

This house can be built on a lot 25 feet wide.

Complete Warm Air Heating Plant, for soft coal, extra	$ 45.43
Complete Warm Air Heating Plant, for hard coal, extra	48.16
Complete Steam Heating Plant, extra	95.30
Complete Hot Water Heating Plant, extra	101.84

Hancock, Wis.

Sears, Roebuck and Co., Chicago, Ill.

Gentlemen:—I will say that on what building material I have bought of you I have saved from 25 to 35 per cent. As to the quality, all I ever got was first class, right up to the grade. I have been well pleased with prompt service.

Yours truly, GEO. DILL.

SEARS, ROEBUCK AND CO.  CHICAGO, ILLINOIS

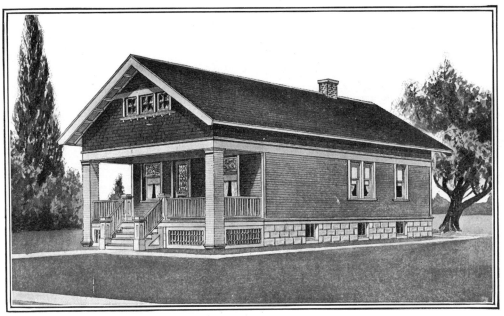

MODERN HOME No. 147

$812.00

For $812.00 we will furnish all the material to build this Six-Room Bungalow, consisting of Mill Work, Siding, Flooring, Ceiling, Finishing Lumber, Building Paper, Pipe, Gutter, Sash Weights, Hardware, Painting Material, Lumber, Lath and Shingles. **NO EXTRAS**, as we guarantee enough material at the above price to build this house according to our plans.

By allowing a fair price for labor, cement, brick and plaster, which we do not furnish, this house can be built for about $1,530.00, including all material and labor.

For Our Offer of Free Plans See Page 3.

AN ATTRACTIVE cottage of frame construction of a popular design, consisting of five rooms and bath and bordering on the bungalow style of architecture. Our architect has taken pains to arrange for good light and ventilation in every room. Different from the ordinary house, it has a large porch 8 feet wide extending across the front of the house, covered by the projection of the upper story and supported with massive built up square columns which are in harmony with the general lines of the house. Unique triple window in the attic and fancy leaded art glass windows add much to this pleasing design.

Leading from the front vestibule, which is 4x5 feet, one enters a large living room 11 feet 6 inches by 14 feet. Living room has a nook, size 7x5 feet, with cased opening, which can be used as a reading room. Living room leads directly to dining room, size 11x13 feet. Directly back of dining room is a good size kitchen, size 11 feet by 10 feet 10 inches, with combination cupboard which opens from both dining room and kitchen sides, a very convenient arrangement. This cupboard facing dining room has four china closet doors glazed with leaded crystal glass, and three large drawers and two small drawers which can be opened from either the dining room or kitchen sides, also two small cupboard doors at the side of the drawers. The kitchen side of the cabinet has six paneled cupboard doors and four small doors above. Double swinging door between dining room and kitchen. Dining room has plate rail. Kitchen has glass door leading to rear porch and door leading to back chamber. To the left of the kitchen is a good size bedroom with entrance to small hall, bathroom and living room. Directly in front is a chamber, size 11x10 feet, with large front window glazed with leaded art glass.

Front door made of veneered birch 1¾ inches thick, glazed with leaded art glass. All inside doors two-panel birch with clear birch trim, such as casing, baseboards, molding, etc., to match. All floors are made of clear yellow pine flooring laid on sub floor.

Built on concrete block foundation and basement excavated under the entire house and has a cement floor.

Framing timbers of No. 1 yellow pine. All outside walls covered with 1-inch dressed and matched sheathing boards and lined with heavy building paper and sided with clear cypress bevel siding on the first story and *A* cedar shingles above first story line and on the roof.

Basement, 7 feet from floor to joists. First floor, 9 feet from floor to ceiling.

Painted with two coats best paint on the outside. Varnish and wood filler for two coats for interior finish.

This house can be built on a lot 27 feet wide.

Complete Warm Air Heating Plant, for soft coal, extra	$ 53.96
Complete Warm Air Heating Plant, for hard coal, extra	55.60
Complete Hot Water Heating Plant, extra	140.82
Complete Steam Heating Plant, extra	115.84
Complete Plumbing Outfit, extra	92.50

SEARS, ROEBUCK AND CO.  **CHICAGO, ILLINOIS**

FLOOR PLAN

GREATER ECONOMY=BIGGER PROFITS

BY BUILDING TWO OR MORE HOUSES AT THE SAME TIME.   ALL LIVE REAL ESTATE OPERATORS AND CONTRACTORS ARE NOW BUILDING ON A LARGER SCALE WHEREVER POSSIBLE.

DO LIKE THE LARGEST REAL ESTATE OPERATORS ARE NOW DOING. Improve your property by building on a little larger scale and reap the big benefits either in the way of increasing your profits or doubling percentage of earnings on your investment. Houses built one at a time under ordinary conditions which would earn you 10 per cent would easily earn you 15 or 50 per cent more profit if the same quality of house was built six at one time.

THERE ARE MANY REASONS WHY YOU CAN LOWER YOUR BUILDING COSTS by this procedure. Here are just a few illustrations. For instance, excavating. While laborers, horses, scoops and other utensils are on the ground, six basements can be excavated at a slight advance over a lesser number. As much as 25 per cent can be saved on this procedure alone. The cost of foundation walls, especially when made of concrete, can be considerably reduced in price when the forms for concrete work can be used for a number of houses, as the cost of lumber for making the forms, and the labor, can be entirely saved for all additional houses, and by placing a larger order for concrete or masonry work, any up to date contractor is willing to make big concessions in price.

BUILDING ON A LARGER SCALE enables the various contractors and sub-contractors to proceed from one building to the next without loss or delay. Carpenters can lay out their framing work for six houses at one time. While one house is in the course of framing, another house will be under its roof, and carpenters during inclement weather can always be worked to the very best possible advantage, which means low building cost for carpenter labor. Plasterers and painters proceed in a like manner, all of them doing the work to the very best advantage and at the very lowest cost. Furthermore, much closer supervision can be had when a number of houses are built close together at one time, as the contractor or foreman can carefully watch the work as it progresses, making every penny paid for labor count to the very best advantage.

WE ARE SELLING MANY OF THE HOUSES SHOWN IN THIS BOOK in lots of fifteen to twenty-five houses, all of which are built in numbers of five to ten at one time. Realty operators and contractors building in this manner claim an actual saving of from 10 to 25 per cent, and claim to give the owner far better satisfaction than would be possible if building one house at a time. On the following pages 90 and 91 we show these very same houses separately with a larger illustration and quote a total price for all the material to complete these houses. In designing these houses it has been our aim to have Modern Homes No. 193, No. 194 and No. 196, with foundations of exactly the same dimensions, thus enabling a contractor when laying out his work and making his form, to use the same forms on the three different houses, all different in design from an exterior viewpoint yet similar in foundation and arrangement on the inside. We also have planned Modern Homes No. 192, No. 195 and No. 197 in a similar manner, which enables realty operators or individuals who are building on a larger scale for the purpose of renting, speculation or selling, to do the work in the most economical manner at the very lowest possible cost and still be in position to erect the six houses one next to the other without being confronted with the monotony that is found in many localities where the same scheme has been followed out, by making slight changes in the front elevation, but not sufficient to make the house look as though each one was an entirely different pattern or design, as we aim to do, and as illustrated above. The above illustration shows six modern homes shown on pages 90 and 91 erected one next to the other on adjoining lots. One can see at a glance that there is no monotony or similarity in their appearance, yet they are constructed on similar foundations and three of each have identical interior arrangements.

IMPROVE YOUR VACANT PROPERTY. If you adopt this scheme of building two or more houses at a time your houses will be sold long before they are completed or, if rented, they will double the interest on your money. Investments of this kind are readily financed by banking institutions or money lenders, as they realize that the security is the best that can be had.

DON'T FORGET that when building in this manner you are cutting out all delays, you are saving in the cost of bringing the scaffolding and utensils from one job to the other, you are practically building six houses with the same amount of trouble and attention that is necessary when building one.

TO THOSE WHO ONLY WANT TO BUILD ONE HOUSE FOR RESIDENCE OR OTHER PURPOSES, you can make no mistake in selecting any one of the designs on the following pages. Each one of them is considered very good, of a convenient arrangement, and the excellent material used puts these houses on a par with any other house we show in this book. We simply have pointed out the advantages of building more than one house at a time, which is now being practiced by all the largest and most up to date realty operators in this country.

SEARS, ROEBUCK AND CO.   **CHICAGO, ILLINOIS**

YOUR CHOICE! $599.00 For Material to Build Any One of These Three Houses

MODERN HOME No. 193

All Three Houses on This Page Have Exactly The Same Floor Plan and Interior Arrangement as Shown.

MODERN HOME No. 196

For $599.00 we will furnish all the Lumber, Lath, Shingles, Mill Work, Flooring, Ceiling, Siding, Finishing Lumber, Building Paper, Pipe, Gutter, Sash Weights, Hardware and Painting Material to build the house selected. NO EXTRAS, as we guarantee enough material at the price shown to build any one of these houses according to our plans.

By allowing a fair price for labor, cement, brick and plaster, which we do not furnish, these houses can be built for about $1,250.00 each, including all material and labor.

MODERN HOME No. 194

ONE-HALF WHAT LOCAL DEALERS CHARGE.

SEARS, ROEBUCK AND CO. QUALITY GUARANTEED **CHICAGO, ILLINOIS**

FIRST FLOOR

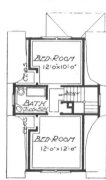

SECOND FLOOR

First Floor.

Hall contains hall seat and open stairway to second floor. Living room is connected with hall and dining room by large cased openings. Kitchen has good pantry 4x5 feet, with pantry case. Stairway from kitchen to cellar is under the stairway to second floor. Front door and rear door are made of best quality white pine, 1⅜ inches thick, glazed with "A" quality double strength glass. Inside doors have four panels, made of best quality yellow pine, 1⅜ inches thick. Clear yellow pine trim and flooring.

Second Floor.

Two bedrooms and bathroom, each bedroom has good size clothes closet. Doors are 1⅛ inches thick, have four panels and are made of yellow pine. Clear yellow pine floors and trim.

Built on a concrete foundation. Sided with narrow clear beveled cypress siding. Cedar shingle roof. All framing timbers of No. 1 yellow pine.

Height of Ceilings.

Cellar, 7 feet from floor to joists.
First floor, 8 feet 6 inches from floor to ceiling.
Second floor, 8 feet from floor to ceiling.
This house can be built on a lot 25 feet wide.

Heating plant or plumbing outfit furnished for any of these houses at the following prices:

Complete Warm Air Heating Plant, for soft coal, extra.	$ 65.43
Complete Warm Air Heating Plant, for hard coal, extra.	68.73
Complete Steam Heating Plant, extra	115.30
Complete Hot Water Heating Plant, extra	138.80
Complete Plumbing Outfit, extra	119.75

YOUR CHOICE! $619⁰⁰ For Material to Build Any One of These Three Houses

MODERN HOME No. 192

MODERN HOME No. 195

MODERN HOME No. 197

All Three Houses on This Page Have Exactly The Same Floor Plan and Interior Arrangement as Shown

FIRST FLOOR

SECOND FLOOR

For $619.00 we will furnish all the Lumber, Lath, Shingles, Mill Work, Flooring, Ceiling, Siding, Finishing Lumber, Building Paper, Pipe, Gutter, Sash Weights, Hardware and Painting Material to build the house selected. NO EXTRAS, as we guarantee enough material at the price shown to build any one of these houses according to our plans.

By allowing a fair price for labor, cement, brick and plaster, which we do not furnish, these houses can be built for about $1,250.00 each, including all material and labor.

First Floor.

Front door opens into large living room. Attractive open stairway of yellow pine across one end of living room. Small hall between living room and dining room. Stairs to basement under main stairway. Kitchen has a good size pantry in which is built a pantry case. Front and rear doors are made of best quality white pine, 1⅜ inches thick, glazed with "A" quality double strength glass. Interior doors are 1⅜ inches thick, have four panels and are made of yellow pine. Clear yellow pine trim and floors.

Second Floor.

Two bedrooms and bathroom, each bedroom has a large clothes closet. Doors are 1⅛ inches thick, made of yellow pine in four-panel design. Yellow pine floors and trim.

Built on a concrete foundation; excavated under entire house. Sided with narrow beveled cypress siding. Cedar shingle roof. Framing timbers of No. 1 yellow pine.

Height of Ceilings.

Cellar, 7 feet from floor to joists. Second floor, 8 feet 6 inches from floor to ceiling. First floor, 8 feet 6 inches from floor to ceiling.

Can be built on a lot 25 feet wide.

Heating plant or plumbing outfit furnished for either of these houses at the following prices:

Complete Warm Air Heating Plant, for soft coal, extra.	$ 63.47
Complete Warm Air Heating Plant, for hard coal, extra.	66.79
Complete Steam Heating Plant, extra.	124.60
Complete Hot Water Heating Plant, extra.	144.21
Complete Plumbing Outfit, extra.	122.70

SEARS, ROEBUCK AND CO.

CHICAGO, ILLINOIS

MODERN HOME No. 64

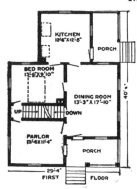

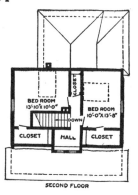

For $622.00 we will furnish all the material to build this Six-Room Concrete Block House, consisting of Mill Work, Flooring, Ceiling, Finishing Lumber, Roofing, Pipe, Gutter, Sash Weights, Hardware, Painting Material, Lumber and Lath. NO EXTRAS, as we guarantee enough material at the above price to build this house according to our plans.

By allowing a fair price for labor, concrete blocks, brick and plaster, which we do not furnish, this house can be built for about $1,710.00, including all material and labor.

For Our Offer of Free Plans See Page 3.

First Floor.

Two entrances from front porch. Parlor and dining room door opening onto porch are clear white pine, 1¾ inches thick, glazed with sand blast design glass. Stairs to basement under main stairway. Rear door made of clear white pine, 1⅜ inches thick, glazed with sand blast design glass. Interior doors have five-cross yellow pine panels with white pine stiles. Clear yellow pine trim. No. 1 yellow pine flooring. Box stairway to second floor.

Second Floor.

Two bedrooms, hall and three closets. Doors are four-panel, 1⅜ inches thick, made with white pine stiles and yellow pine panels. Clear yellow pine trim. No. 1 yellow pine flooring.

Outside woodwork painted two coats. Varnish and wood filler for two coats of interior finish.

Excavated basement under the entire house, 7 feet from floor to joists, with cement floor. Rooms on the first floor are 9 feet 2 inches from floor to ceiling; rooms on the second floor, 8 feet 8 inches from floor to ceiling.

This house can be built on a lot 36 feet wide.

Complete Warm Air Heating Plant, for soft coal, extra	$ 62.16
Complete Warm Air Heating Plant, for hard coal, extra	65.38
Complete Hot Water Heating Plant, extra	162.95

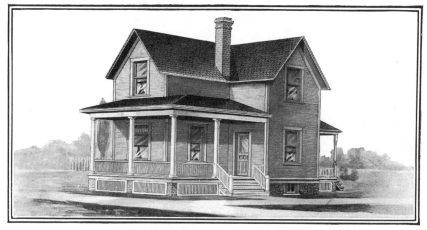

MODERN HOME No. 104

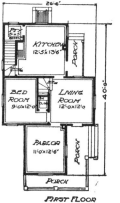

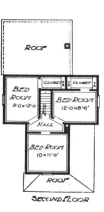

For $689.00 we will furnish all the material to build this Seven-Room House, consisting of Mill Work, Ceiling, Siding, Flooring, Finishing Lumber, Building Paper, Pipe, Gutter, Sash Weights, Hardware, Painting Material, Lumber, Lath and Shingles. NO EXTRAS, as we guarantee enough material at the above price to build this house according to our plans.

By allowing a fair price for labor, stone, brick and plaster, which we do not furnish, this house can be built for about $1,550.00, including all material and labor.

For Our Offer of Free Plans See Page 3.

First Floor.

Four rooms and pantry. Front door is made of clear white pine, 1⅜ inches thick, glazed with sand blast design glass. Interior doors and rear door are five-panel, 1⅜ inches thick, and made of clear yellow pine. Clear yellow pine trim. No. 1 yellow pine flooring. Box stairway from living room to second floor.

Second Floor.

Three bedrooms, two closets and hall. Doors have five panels, made of clear yellow pine and are 1⅜ inches thick, with clear yellow pine trim to match. No. 1 yellow pine floors.

Painted two coats outside; your choice of color. Varnish and wood filler for interior finish.

Built on a stone foundation, frame construction, sided with narrow bevel edge cypress siding and has cedar shingle roof.

Excavated basement under the entire house, 6 feet 6 inches from floor to joists. Rooms on first floor, 8 feet 6 inches from floor to ceiling; second floor, 8 feet 4 inches from floor to ceiling.

This house measures 26 feet 6 inches wide by 40 feet long and can be built on a lot 27 feet 6 inches wide.

Complete Warm Air Heating Plant, for soft coal, extra	$ 65.10
Complete Warm Air Heating Plant, for hard coal, extra	68.31
Complete Steam Heating Plant, extra	137.45

MODERN HOME No. 70

$517⁰⁰

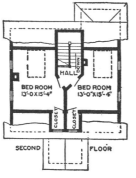

For $517.00 we will furnish all the Mill Work, Flooring, Ceiling, Finishing Lumber, Pipe, Gutter, Sash Weights, Hardware, Painting Material, Lumber, Lath and Shingles for this Six-Room House. NO EXTRAS, as we guarantee enough material at the above price to build this house according to our plans.

By allowing a fair price for labor, concrete blocks and plaster, which we do not furnish, this house can be built for about $1,400.00, including all material and labor.

For Our Offer of Free Plans See Page 3.

A CONCRETE block house with a good size living room and cased opening between the living room and dining room. Kitchen and bedroom on the first floor and two large bedrooms on the second floor with two closets. Inside cellar way to the basement under the main stairs. Front porch, 8x8 feet, with Colonial columns; rear porch, 11x5 feet.

Front door glazed with figured design glass. First floor inside doors are five-cross panel with soft pine stiles and rails and yellow pine panels. Second floor inside doors are four-panel clear soft pine. Yellow pine baseboard, casing and trim throughout the house. No. 1 yellow pine flooring for the entire house and porches.

All windows glazed with "A" quality glass. All windows throughout the house hung on sash weights.

Excavated basement under the entire house, 7 feet high. Rooms on the first floor are 8 feet 6 inches from floor to ceiling; second floor, 8 feet from floor to ceiling.

This house can be built on a lot 32 feet wide.

Complete Warm Air Heating Plant, for soft coal, extra..$ 64.75
Complete Warm Air Heating Plant, for hard coal, extra.. 68.76
Complete Steam Heating Plant, extra................... 118.65
Complete Hot Water Heating Plant, extra.............. 131.72

MODERN HOME No. 125

$724⁰⁰

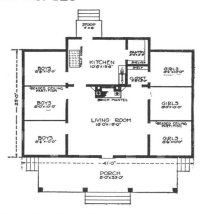

For $724.00 we will furnish Mill Work, Flooring, Ceiling, Siding, Finishing Lumber, Roofing, Building Paper, Pipe, Gutter, Sash Weights, Hardware, Painting Material and Lumber for this Eight-Room Bungalow. NO EXTRAS, as we guarantee enough material at the above price to build this house according to our plans.

By allowing a fair price for labor and brick, which we do not furnish, this house can be built for about $1,040.00, including all material and labor.

For Our Offer of Free Plans See Page 3.

A N IDEAL cottage for a summer home or water edge resort. Has a large porch across the front of the house, 33 feet by 8 feet, with Colonial columns; overhanging roof.

By referring to the floor plan you will notice the large living room, 16x19 feet, with doors leading to four of the side bedrooms and to the kitchen. The three bedrooms on each side are separated with beaded wood partition. In the living room is a brick rustic mantel and fireplace.

Front door glazed with leaded glass. Inside doors clear soft wood and clear soft wood molding and trim. No. 1 yellow pine flooring throughout the entire house and porch.

Built on a frame foundation with 8x8-inch girders. Frame construction, sided with narrow bevel edge cypress siding and has Best-of-all Roofing.

Painted two coats outside; your choice of color. Varnish and wood filler for interior finish.

Cellar, 10x18 feet, 6 feet from floor to joists. Rooms on the main floor are 10 feet from floor to ceiling.

This house can be built on a lot 46 feet wide.

Complete Warm Air Heating Plant, for soft coal, extra..$ 71.73
Complete Warm Air Heating Plant, for hard coal, extra.. 74.31
Complete Hot Water Heating Plant, extra.............. 163.35
Complete Steam Heating Plant, extra................. 121.80

SEARS, ROEBUCK AND CO. QUALITY GUARANTEED **CHICAGO, ILLINOIS**

MODERN HOME No. 183

MODERN HOME No. 186

NO EXTRAS, as we guarantee enough material at the prices to build these houses according to our plans.

For $745.00 we will furnish all the material to build this Five-Room Cottage, consisting of Lumber, Lath, Shingles, Mill Work, Ceiling, Siding, Flooring, Finishing Lumber, Building Paper, Pipe, Gutter, Sash Weights, Hardware and Painting Material.

By allowing a fair price for labor, cement, brick and plaster, which we do not furnish, this house can be built for about $1,500.00, including all material and labor.

For Our Offer of Free Plans See Page 3.

A NEAT five-room cottage of conventional design, with bath. Front door is made of clear white pine, 1¾ inches thick, glazed with bevel plate glass. Colonnade between living room and dining room. Buffet in dining room. Inside doors five-cross panel, clear yellow pine, with yellow pine trim to match. Oak floor in the living room and dining room. Maple floor in the balance of the house. Bedrooms have clothes closets; windows in each closet. Kitchen has a pantry in which is built a pantry case of drawers. Large unfinished attic, could be converted into two good rooms at a slight expense.

Built on a concrete foundation, basement under the entire house. We furnish clear cypress siding and cedar shingles. Framing timbers are of the best quality yellow pine.
Basement has cement floor and is 7 feet from floor to joists. First floor 9 feet from floor to ceiling. Painted with two coats of the best paint outside. Varnish and wood filler for the interior finish.

This house can be built on a lot 25 feet wide.

Complete Warm Air Heating Plant, for soft coal, extra.	$ 52.92
Complete Warm Air Heating Plant, for hard coal, extra.	56.24
Complete Steam Heating Plant, extra	104.50
Complete Hot Water Heating Plant, extra	129.53
Complete Plumbing Outfit, extra	114.05

FIRST FLOOR PLAN

For $682.00 we will furnish all the material to build this Six-Room Cottage, consisting of Lumber, Lath, Shingles, Mill Work, Flooring, Ceiling, Siding, Finishing Lumber, Building Paper, Pipe, Gutter, Sash Weights, Hardware and Painting Material.

By allowing a fair price for labor, cement, brick and plaster, which we do not furnish, this house can be built for about $1,375.00, including all material and labor.

For Our Offer of Free Plans See Page 3.

AN ATTRACTIVE home of six rooms and bath. Has open stairway in the living room, a large buffet in the dining room and pantry in which is built a pantry case.

First Floor.
Front door of clear white pine, 1¾ inches thick, glazed with double strength glass sand blast design. Inside doors are five-panel clear yellow pine. Clear yellow pine floor and trim. Rear door clear white pine, 1⅜ inches thick, glazed with clear glass.

Second Floor.
Stairway to second floor leads to hall. Bedrooms have good size closets. Large closet extending entire length of house for storage purposes. Doors are four-panel clear yellow pine, with yellow pine trim and floors to match.
Built on a concrete block foundation, excavated under the entire house, with cement floor in the basement. We furnish clear cypress siding and cedar shingles.
Basement, 7 feet from floor to joists. First floor, 9 feet from floor to ceiling. Second floor, 8 feet 6 inches from floor to ceiling. Painted with two coats of the best paint outside. Varnish and wood filler for interior finish.

This house can be built on a lot 25 feet wide.

Complete Warm Air Heating Plant, for soft coal, extra.	$ 63.05
Complete Warm Air Heating Plant, for hard coal, extra.	66.25
Complete Steam Heating Plant, extra	122.85
Complete Hot Water Heating Plant, extra	153.76
Complete Plumbing Outfit, extra	116.75

FIRST FLOOR PLAN

SECOND FLOOR PLAN

SEARS, ROEBUCK AND CO.

QUALITY GUARANTEED

CHICAGO, ILLINOIS

MODERN HOME No. 36

$702.00

FIRST FLOOR

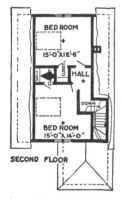

SECOND FLOOR

For $702.00 we will furnish all Lumber, Lath and Shingles, the Mill Work, Ceiling, Siding, Flooring, Finishing Lumber, Building Paper, Pipe, Gutter, Sash Weights, Hardware, and Painting Material for this Six-Room Cottage. NO EXTRAS, as we guarantee enough material at the above price to build this house according to our plans.

By allowing a fair price for labor, cement, brick and plaster, which we do not furnish, this house can be built for about $1,350.00, including all material and labor.

For Our Offer of Free Plans See Page 3.

A LARGE, well built cottage with all available space made good use of. A large living room with cased opening leading into the hall; also cased opening between the living room and dining room. One bedroom on the first floor; two large bedrooms on the second floor.

Front door, 1¾ inches thick, glazed with bevel plate glass. Queen Anne windows for the reception hall; twin Queen Anne windows for front bedroom on the second floor; cottage window with lace design glass for the front window in the living room. Interior trim consists of clear yellow pine casing, base and molding. Open stairway leading from reception hall.

Built on a concrete foundation, frame construction, sided with narrow bevel clear cypress siding with cedar shingle roof and gables. Porch, 8x10 feet.

Painted outside two coats; choice of color. Varnish and wood filler for two coats of interior finish.

Excavated basement, 7 feet from floor to joists. Rooms on first floor, 9 feet from floor to ceiling; rooms on second floor, 8 feet from floor to ceiling.

This house can be built on a lot 27 feet wide.

Complete Warm Air Heating Plant, for soft coal, extra.$ 70.96
Complete Warm Air Heating Plant, for hard coal, extra. 74.24
Complete Steam Heating Plant, extra.................. 123.37
Complete Hot Water Heating Plant, extra............. 169.97

MODERN HOME No. 106

$591.00

FIRST FLOOR PLAN

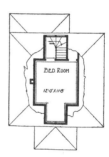

SECOND FLOOR PLAN

For $591.00 we will furnish all Lumber, Lath and Shingles, the Mill Work, Siding, Ceiling, Finishing Lumber, Building Paper, Pipe, Gutter, Sash Weights, Hardware, and Painting Material for this Five-Room House. NO EXTRAS, as we guarantee enough material at the above price to build this house according to our plans.

By allowing a fair price for labor, stone, brick and plaster, which we do not furnish, this house can be built for about $1,250.00, including all material and labor.

For Our Offer of Free Plans See Page 3.

A ONE-STORY COTTAGE with attic finished into one large room. Four rooms on the first floor. Cellar stairs directly under the main stairs leading from the kitchen. Outside cellar entrance. Good size pantry and closet. Marginal light attic sash. Two good size windows in each room on the first floor and four sash in the room in the attic.

Five-cross panel interior doors, soft pine stiles and rails, yellow pine panels. Clear yellow pine trim, moldings and stairs. No. 1 yellow pine flooring throughout the entire house and porches.

Built on a stone foundation, frame construction, sided with narrow bevel clear cypress siding and has cedar shingle roof. Colonial porch columns.

Painted two coats outside; your choice of color. Varnish and wood filler for interior finish.

Excavated basement under the entire house, 6 feet 10 inches from floor to joists. Rooms on the first floor are 8 feet 6 inches from floor to ceiling; second floor, 8 feet from floor to ceiling.

This house measures 29 feet 6 inches long by 26 feet wide and can be built on a lot 30 feet wide.

Complete Warm Air Heating Plant, for soft coal, extra.$ 53.65
Complete Warm Air Heating Plant, for hard coal, extra. 56.91
Complete Hot Water Heating Plant, extra............. 130.37
Complete Steam Heating Plant, extra................. 110.02

SEARS, ROEBUCK AND CO.  CHICAGO, ILLINOIS

MODERN HOME No. 134

$528⁰⁰

FLOOR PLAN

For $528.00 we will furnish all the material to build this Four-Room Cottage, consisting of Mill Work, Flooring, Ceiling, Finishing Lumber, Building Paper, Pipe, Gutter, Sash Weights, Hardware, Painting Material, Lumber, Lath and Shingles. NO EXTRAS, as we guarantee enough material at the above price to build this house according to our plans.

By allowing a fair price for labor, cement, brick and plaster, which we do not furnish, this house can be built for about $1,220.00, including all material and labor.

By using bevel siding instead of stonekote this house can be built for about $1,140.00 including all material and labor.

We will furnish cypress bevel siding for this house at $36.00 extra. We do not furnish stonekote.

For Our Offer of Free Plans See Page 3.

THIS cottage has four rooms and quite a large attic which could very easily be finished into two rooms if desired.

Monroe front and rear doors. All inside doors are five-cross panel with soft pine stiles and rails, yellow pine panels. Clear yellow pine trim. Clear yellow pine flooring for the entire house and porches.

Built on a concrete foundation, frame construction, sided with stonekote, more commonly known as cement plaster, or cypress bevel siding, and has cedar shingle roof.

Varnish and wood filler for two coats of interior finish.

Excavated basement under the entire house, 6 feet 6 inches from floor to joists. Rooms on the main floor are 9 feet from floor to ceiling.

This house can be built on a lot 25 feet wide.

Complete Warm Air Heating Plant, for soft coal, extra.$	48.73
Complete Warm Air Heating Plant, for hard coal, extra.	51.35
Complete Steam Heating Plant, extra...................	99.55
Complete Hot Water Heating Plant, extra..............	119.17
Complete Plumbing Outfit, extra......................	100.63

SEARS, ROEBUCK AND CO.

QUALITY GUARANTEED

CHICAGO, ILLINOIS

MODERN HOME No. 139

$449⁰⁰

For $449.00 we will furnish all the material to build this Four-Room Cottage, consisting of Mill Work, Flooring, Ceiling, Finishing Lumber, Building Paper, Pipe, Gutter, Sash Weights, Hardware, Painting Material, Lumber, Lath and Shingles. NO EXTRAS, as we guarantee enough material at the above price to build this house according to our plans.

By allowing a fair price for labor, cement, brick and plaster, which we do not furnish, this house can be built for about $1,075.00, including all material and labor.

By using bevel siding instead of stonekote this house can be built for about $1,000.00, including all material and labor.

We will furnish cypress bevel siding for this house at $35.00 extra. We do not furnish stonekote.

For Our Offer of Free Plans See Page 3.

AN ATTRACTIVE little cottage, sided with stonekote. Bay window on the front, with colored leaded art glass front window and Queen Anne attic sash. Front porch, 6 feet by 11 feet 6 inches; rear porch, 5x4 feet. Front door opens directly into large living room which has a door leading to the kitchen and one to the side bedroom. The kitchen being large is used as combination kitchen and dining room. Good size pantry. The attic is quite high and could easily be finished off into sleeping rooms if desired.

Front door glazed with lace design glass. Rear door glazed with clear glass. Clear soft pine doors for the interior, clear yellow pine molding and trim. Clear yellow pine flooring throughout the entire house and porches. Varnish and wood filler for two coats of interior finish.

Built on a concrete foundation, frame construction, sided with stonekote or cypress bevel siding, and has cedar shingle roof.

Rooms on the main floor are 9 feet from floor to ceiling.

This house can be built on a lot 25 feet 6 inches wide.

Floor Plan.

Complete Warm Air Heating Plant, for soft coal, extra.$	50.33
Complete Warm Air Heating Plant, for hard coal, extra.	53.70
Complete Steam Heating Plant, extra...................	103.35
Complete Hot Water Heating Plant, extra..............	128.33
Complete Plumbing Outfit, extra......................	100.63

MODERN HOME No. 152

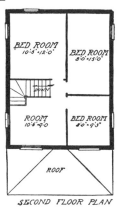

FIRST FLOOR PLAN

For **$360.00** we will furnish all the Mill Work, Flooring, Ceiling, Finishing Lumber, Pipe, Gutter, Sash Weights, Roofing, Hardware and Painting Material, Lumber and Lath for this Eight-Room House. NO EXTRAS, as we guarantee enough material at the above price to build this house according to our plans.

By allowing a fair price for labor, concrete blocks, brick and plaster, which we do not furnish, this house can be built for about $770.00, including all material and labor.

SECOND FLOOR PLAN

For Our Offer of Free Plans See Page 3.

First Floor.
Front door of white pine, 1⅜ inches thick, opens into living room. Open stairway in living room. Well lighted pantry in kitchen. Interior doors and back door made with four panels of solid yellow pine. Clear yellow pine trim. No. 1 yellow pine floors. Plastered throughout.

Second Floor.
Stairs open on landing, from which any of the bedrooms may be entered. Solid yellow pine doors with four panels. Cement wall plastered. Beaded wood partition of No. 1 yellow pine between rooms. Queen Anne sash for two front rooms. No. 1 yellow pine floors. Roofed with Best-of-all Roofing.

Built on a concrete foundation. First floor, 9 feet from floor to ceiling. Second floor, 8 feet from floor to ceiling. Outside woodwork painted two coats. Varnish and wood filler for interior finish.

This house can be built on a lot 25 feet wide.

Complete Warm Air Heating Plant, for soft coal, extra..$	62.73
Complete Warm Air Heating Plant, for hard coal, extra..	66.53
Complete Steam Heating Plant, extra...................	132.62
Complete Hot Water Heating Plant, extra...........	166.12

SEARS, ROEBUCK AND CO.

QUALITY GUARANTEED

CHICAGO, ILLINOIS

—97—

MODERN HOME No. 136

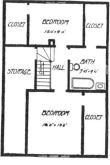

FIRST FLOOR PLAN

SECOND FLOOR PLAN

For **$708.00** we will furnish all the material to build this Six-Room House, consisting of Mill Work, Siding, Flooring, Ceiling, Finishing Lumber, Building Paper, Pipe, Gutter, Sash Weights, Hardware, Painting Material, Lumber, Lath and Shingles. NO EXTRAS, as we guarantee enough material at the above price to build this house according to our plans.

By allowing a fair price for labor, cement, brick and plaster, which we do not furnish, this house can be built for about $1,435.00 including all material and labor.

For Our Offer of Free Plans See Page 3.

First Floor.
Front door is of clear white pine, 1⅜ inches thick, glazed with leaded art glass, opens into reception hall. Reception hall has yellow pine open stairway. Single sliding door between hall and parlor. Dining room has cupboard built in. Kitchen has well lighted pantry, and a closet. Interior doors, 1⅜ inches thick with clear white pine stiles and five yellow pine panels. Rear door, 1⅜ inches thick, made of clear white pine, glazed with lace design glass. Clear yellow pine trim and floors.

Second Floor.
Stairway opens into small hall. Two bedrooms, bathroom, three closets and a large storage closet. Doors have five yellow pine panels with white pine stiles. Clear yellow pine trim and floors.

Built on a concrete block foundation, frame construction, sided with narrow bevel edge cypress siding; gables and roof shingled with cedar shingles.

Excavated basement under the entire house, 6 feet 6 inches from floor to joists, with cement floor. Rooms on the first floor are 9 feet from floor to ceiling; second floor, 8 feet from floor to ceiling.

This house can be built on a lot 26 feet wide.

Complete Warm Air Heating Plant, for soft coal, extra..$	76.00
Complete Warm Air Heating Plant, for hard coal, extra..	79.00
Complete Steam Heating Plant, extra..................	122.85
Complete Hot Water Heating Plant, extra.............	156.91
Complete Plumbing Outfit, extra......................	104.72

MODERN HOME No. 400

$373⁰⁰

For $373.00 we will furnish all the material to build this Four-Room Bungalow, consisting of Lumber, Lath, Shingles, Mill Work, Ceiling, Siding, Flooring, Finishing Lumber, Building Paper, Pipe, Gutter, Sash Weights, Hardware and Painting Material. NO EXTRAS, as we guarantee enough material at the above price to build this house according to our plans.

By allowing a fair price for labor, cement, brick and plaster, which we do not furnish, this bungalow can be built for about $750.00, including all material and labor.

For Our Offer of Free Plans See Page 3.

IN BUNGALOW No. 400 we offer a house at a low price with an absolute guarantee as to the quality of the materials we furnish. Front door is of veneered oak, 1¾ inches thick, glazed with a sand blast design. All inside doors have five panels, made of yellow pine with yellow pine trim to match. All floors are of clear yellow pine. Both bedrooms have good size clothes closets. The kitchen has a large well lighted pantry.

Built on a concrete foundation, not excavated. Frame construction and sided with narrow beveled clear cypress siding. Roofed with cedar shingles. All framing timbers are of the best quality yellow pine.

Painted two coats of best paint outside, your choice of color. Varnish and wood filler for two coats of interior finish. Rooms are 8 feet 4 inches from floor to ceiling.

This house can be built on a lot 25 feet wide.

MODERN HOME No. 401

$483⁰⁰

For $483.00 we will furnish all the material to build this Five-Room Bungalow, consisting of Mill Work, Lumber, Lath, Shingles, Ceiling, Siding, Flooring, Finishing Lumber, Building Paper, Pipe, Gutter, Sash Weights, Hardware and Painting Material. NO EXTRAS, as we guarantee enough material at the above price to build this house according to our plans.

By allowing a fair price for labor, brick, cement and plaster, which we do not furnish, this house can be built for about $950.00, including all material and labor.

For Our Offer of Free Plans See Page 3.

A BUNGALOW of tasty design. All material is of guaranteed quality. A porch extends across the entire front. The front door is of veneered oak, 1¾ inches thick, glazed with sand blast design glass. The parlor and dining room are each 11 feet 3 inches by 13 feet 3 inches and are divided by a large cased opening. Each bedroom has a wardrobe. All interior doors are of the five-panel design, made of the best quality yellow pine, with yellow pine trim to match. All floors are of clear yellow pine.

Built on a concrete block foundation; frame construction. Sided with narrow beveled clear cypress siding. Cedar shingles furnished for the roof.

Painted two coats of the best paint outside, varnished and wood filler for two coats of interior finish; 8 feet 4 inches from floor to ceiling.

This house can be built on a lot 30 feet wide.

SEARS, ROEBUCK AND CO.  CHICAGO, ILLINOIS

MODERN HOME No. 107

For $398.00 we will furnish all the Mill Work, Flooring, Ceiling, Siding, Finishing Lumber, Building Paper, Pipe, Gutter, Sash Weights, Hardware and Painting Material, Lumber, Lath and Shingles to build this Three-Room Cottage. NO EXTRAS, as we guarantee enough material at the above price to build this house according to our plans.

By allowing a fair price for labor, cement, brick and plaster, which we do not furnish, this house can be built for about $972.00, including all material and labor.

For Our Offer of Free Plans See Page 3.

— FLOOR PLAN —

THIS cottage has three good size rooms with pantry and closet. Front porch, 13 feet by 4 feet 6 inches; rear porch, 6x5 feet. Outside cellar entrance.

Leaded Crystal front window in the living room. All other windows are glazed with "A" quality double strength glass with the exception of the pantry window which is glazed with single strength glass.

Cass front door. Inside doors are five-panel solid yellow pine. Clear yellow pine molding and trim. No. 1 yellow pine flooring, cypress siding and cedar shingles.

This is just the type of cottage that is being put up in large numbers by factory or mine owners who furnish their employes with cottages, and in that case it is sometimes built on a frame foundation instead of stone, which reduces the cost about $180.00, thereby making a very good paying investment.

Excavated basement under the entire house, 6 feet from floor to joists. Rooms on the main floor are 8 feet 6 inches from floor to ceiling.

This house is 20 feet 6 inches wide by 31 feet long and can be built on a lot 22 feet 6 inches wide

Complete Warm Air Heating Plant, for soft coal, extra...................................$42.14
Complete Warm Air Heating Plant, for hard coal, extra................................... 45.40

MODERN HOME No. 142

For $282.00 we will furnish all the Mill Work, Flooring, Siding, Finishing Lumber, Building Paper, Eaves Trough, Roofing, Hardware, Painting Material, Lumber and Lath to build this Four-Room House. NO EXTRAS, as we guarantee enough material at the above price to build this house according to our plans.

By allowing a fair price for labor, brick and plaster, which we do not furnish, this house can be built for about $545.00, including all material and labor.

For Our Offer of Free Plans See Page 3.

A GOOD and well built cottage with four rooms, two closets and pantry. We furnish the same high standard quality of material for this cottage as we do for the higher priced houses shown in this book.

One of our high grade grained doors for the front. All windows with the exception of the pantry window glazed with "A" quality double strength glass. Clear yellow pine molding and trim. Clear yellow pine flooring.

Built on a frame foundation, frame construction and sided with narrow bevel edge cypress siding. Three and one-half-ply Best-of-all Felt Roofing. Plastered two coats inside. Painted two coats outside; your choice of color. Varnish and wood filler for two coats of interior finish.

Rooms are 8 feet 4 inches from floor to ceiling.

This house can be built on a lot 22 feet 6 inches wide.

Complete Warm Air Heating Plant, for soft coal, extra...................................$45.43
Complete Warm Air Heating Plant, for hard coal, extra................................... 48.05

SEARS, ROEBUCK AND CO.

QUALITY GUARANTEED

CHICAGO, ILLINOIS

SIMPLEX READY

No. 7 $92.00
Garage, size 12 ft. 4 in. by 16 ft.

SIMPLE, STRONG AND ECONOMICAL. We handle a complete line of ready made buildings, garages, chicken houses, photograph galleries and cottages of many sizes, from one room to five rooms, all of which are attractively designed and made in such large quantities that you could hardly buy the material necessary to build one of them for the price we quote you on the complete house, ready to bolt together.

SIMPLEX HOUSES ARE PORTABLE. They can be taken apart as readily as they are put together. Ideal for lakeside or summer resorts. Anyone owning a Simplex portable building can move it from one place to another at little or no expense or store it for future use. Sections are interchangeable, making it possible to lengthen the house at any time by adding other sections.

STRONG AND STURDY enough for any purpose. Many Simplex houses are being used by homesteaders in the West and Northwest for farm houses. They can easily be made warm enough for the most severe weather by lining with Peerless Wall Board, fully described in our Book of Ready Made Buildings.

READ
ABOUT
OUR
LIBERAL
GUARANTEE

No. 10 $155.00
Garage, size 16 ft. by 18 ft.

WE GUARANTEE SAFE DELIVERY and will replace broken glass or make good any damage, providing the customer sends us the paid expense bill with a notation signed by the freight agent, stating the condition of the shipment on its arrival at destination, so that we can use this statement of agent in making claim on the railroad company for damages.

Please remember that the prices quoted on our ready made buildings cover the entire cost of the complete structure, the prices even include screws, bolts and all other necessary hardware; in fact, we furnish everything necessary to erect these houses with the exception of the wrench, hammer and screwdriver.

Complete set of instructions furnished free, showing how the sections (sides, roof and porch) are put together.

No. 8 $169.00
Garage, size 18 ft. by 20 ft. 4 in.

SEARS, ROEBUCK AND CO.

CHICAGO, ILLINOIS

MADE HOUSES AND GARAGES

WHY OUR PRICES ARE SO LOW. The cost of a ready made building depends on the cost of lumber, as half of the entire cost is in this one item alone. We manufacture our own lumber from our own logs in our big Southern mills. Our ready made building factory is operated in connection with our **big 40-acre** lumber yard in Southern Illinois. We are independent of the lumber trust and our method of "from stump to consumer" saves you the jobbers' profit, the wholesale dealers' profit and the retail dealers' profit. We make you a further saving by manufacturing our Simplex Portable Buildings in large quantities at our new modernly equipped factory. All this saving goes to the customer buying a Simplex Ready Made Building in the way of lowering the price and bettering the quality. Shipped from factory in Southern Illinois. We carry a full assortment in stock ready for instant delivery. We can fill your order within five days. Our houses can be put up ready to live in within a few hours. No saw or plane or other tools necessary. The only tools required are a wrench, hammer and screwdriver.

OUR CATALOG OF
Ready Made Buildings
IS FREE

**Ready about February 15th.
Write for it at that time, if interested.**

No. 17 $399.00
Size, 26 ft. 4 in. by 30 ft.   Five rooms.

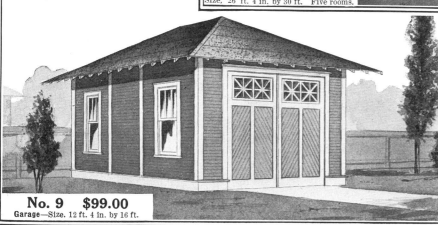

No. 9 $99.00
Garage—Size, 12 ft. 4 in. by 16 ft.

The sketches to the right, Figures 1, 2 and 3 show our 5-room Ready Made House No. 17 ready to bolt together.

Figure 1 shows floor framing and layout of house.

Figure 2 shows the wall sections and location of rooms.

Figure 3 shows the roof sections before the sections are bolted together and before the Oriental Red Slate Roofing is applied.

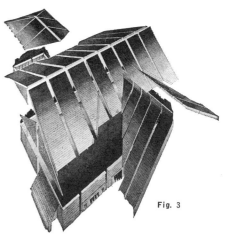

Fig. 3

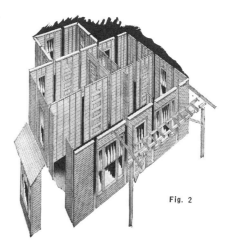

Fig. 2

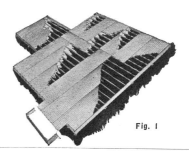

Fig. 1

SEARS, ROEBUCK AND CO.   **CHICAGO, ILLINOIS**

SEARS, ROEBUCK AND CO.'S BIG SAW MILLS LOCATED IN THE HEART OF THE GREAT FORESTS IN THE SOUTH

LIGHT AND POWER PLANT — WARE HOUSES Nº 1-2-3-4 — PLANING MILLS — STEAM DRY KILNS — WARE HOUSES Nº 5 & 6 — LOG TRAIN RAMPS AND LOG POND — LOG AND LUMBER MILLS

Why pay 3 profits? Save from $100⁰⁰ to $150⁰⁰ on Enough Lumber for the Average House or Barn.

Let us prove that we can make you this big saving by shipping a carload of lumber, lath and shingles from our Southern mill or Illinois yards direct to you with but one profit (instead of the usual three profits) added to the lowest manufacturing cost.

Ossining, New York.

Sears, Roebuck and Co., Chicago, Ill.

Dear Sirs:—I put up a house for Mr. James M. Ferguson, he buying the lumber from you. We have offered a reward of one dollar for every knot as large as a 10-cent piece found on this house, but up to the present time no one has asked for a dollar, for the reason that a knot large enough to cover a 10-cent piece cannot be found on the whole house. It is the best lumber I have used in a long while.

Yours truly,

Henry V. Tillotson

189 Spring Street.

STOP PAYING WHOLESALERS' AND RETAILERS' PROFITS. Send for our Wholesale Lumber Price List. It quotes you the lowest wholesale prices, which include freight charges to your station, on a most complete assortment of lumber. We carry a total stock of over 2,500 carloads of lumber, in every length, width and thickness. A stock larger than is carried by a hundred average size lumber yards.

WE SHIP LUMBER QUICK. On account of the enormous stock carried we are able to ship complete orders on a few days' notice from either our big mills in the South or from our big distributing yards in Illinois.

WE GUARANTEE THE QUALITY TO BE SUPERIOR to the kind retail dealers furnish. If our lumber does not prove to be better, return it at our expense and we will cheerfully return your money.

THIS IS OUR **WHOLESALE LUMBER PRICE LIST**

We Publish Special Lumber Price Lists Quoting "Delivered Prices" to Every City in the United States.

Let Us Send You a List Showing Our Delivered Prices (Freight Prepaid) to Your Station. Mailed Free on Request.

If you cannot wait for our delivered Lumber Price List, SEND US YOUR LIST, we will gladly mail you our bid quoting you our prices on your entire bill of lumber or mill work. The prices, however, will be exactly the same as the prices printed in our wholesale price list.

If you contemplate building, be sure to send for this Wholesale Lumber Price List. It is free on request.

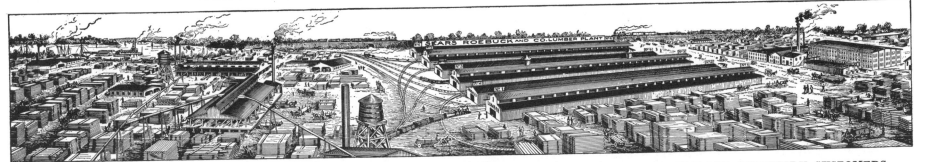

OUR BIG LUMBER PLANT AND YARDS, LOCATED IN ILLINOIS, FROM WHICH POINT WE SHIP TO EASTERN AND NORTHERN CUSTOMERS.

SEARS, ROEBUCK AND CO.

CHICAGO, ILLINOIS

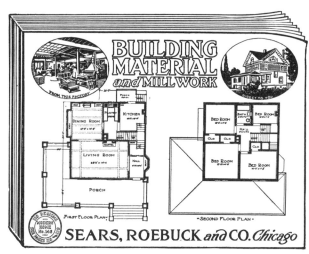

BARN No. 16

$633.00

For $633.00 we will furnish all the material to build this Barn, consisting of Rough Lumber, Framing Timbers, Plank Flooring, Roofing, Hardware, Sash and Paint. NO EXTRAS, as we guarantee enough material at the above price to build this barn according to our plans.

By allowing a fair price for labor, concrete blocks and concrete floors, which we do not supply, this barn may be built for about $925.00, including all material and labor.

For Our Offer of Free Plans See Page 3.

BARN No. 16 is 30 feet wide, 54 feet long and 16 feet high to the eaves. It is built of solid timber construction with gambrel roof. This roof is of the self supporting type and offers no obstruction to the free operation of the hay carrier. Floor plans show six horse stalls arranged across the building and two rows of cow stalls facing a feed alley running at right angles to the horse stable. This space will be found sufficient to comfortably accommodate from sixteen to eighteen head of cattle.

The horse stable is entirely separate from the cattle stable, though one of the stalls may be used for a passage if desired. A stairway is provided in the feed alley leading to the second floor, and the hay chute, as well as the grain chute, are conveniently located so as to reduce the labor of feeding to a minimum. The grain room is on the second floor, extending entirely across one end of the barn. This room will hold a large amount of feed and, if desired, may be subdivided into bins.

The lumber we furnish is No. 1 grade. The 3½-Ply Red Slate Prepared Roofing is guaranteed to last twelve years and looks better than shingles.

We furnish paint sufficient for two-coat work for the exterior woodwork. Your choice of colors.

This barn is built on a concrete block foundation and has concrete floor in all passages and feed alleys.

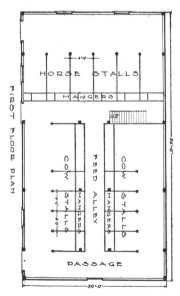

FIRST FLOOR PLAN

For $56.00 we will furnish all the material to build a **lean-to shed**, size 26x16 feet and 12 feet high, which can be built on one end of any barn shown in this book. Blue prints of this shed will be furnished free with the barn plans you order if requested.

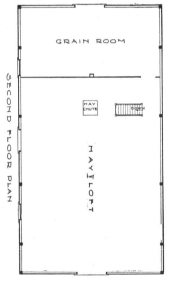

SECOND FLOOR PLAN

SEARS, ROEBUCK AND CO.  **CHICAGO, ILLINOIS**

BARN No. 11

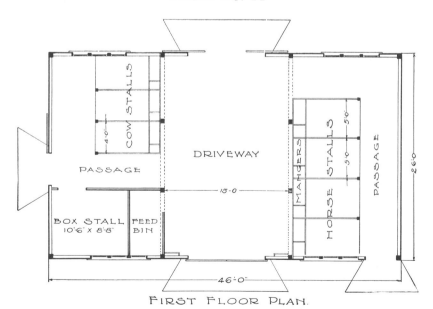

FIRST FLOOR PLAN.

COW STALLS

PASSAGE

DRIVEWAY

MANGERS

HORSE STALLS

PASSAGE

BOX STALL
10'-6" X 8'-8"

FEED BIN

4'-0"

5'-0"

5'-0"

5'-0"

15'-0"

26'-0"

46'-0"

$464⁰⁰

For $464.00 we will furnish all the material to build this Barn, consisting of all the Lumber, Framing Timbers, Plank Flooring for all Horse and Cattle Stalls, Prepared Roofing, Sash, Hardware and Paint.

By allowing a fair price for labor, concrete blocks and concrete floors for passages, which we do not furnish, this barn may be built for about $675.00, including all material and labor.

For Our Offer of Free Plans See Page 3.

THIS barn is 26 feet wide, 46 feet long, and 16 feet to the eaves. It is built of solid timber construction, making it a very substantial building. The roof is of the gambrel type, self supporting, thus allowing free operation of the hay carrier. The floor plan shows four horse stalls and space enough on the other side of the building for three cows in addition to a box stall and feed room. The doors are large enough to permit driving into with a load of hay.

The material we supply for this building is first class in every way. The framing lumber is all No. 1. The Red Slate Surfaced Roofing used on roof is guaranteed to last twelve years and presents a better appearance than shingles.

The paint will be supplied for two coats outside work. Your choice of colors.

The barn is built on a concrete block foundation which should be put deep enough to be below the frost line.

CONTRACTORS CLAIM THE QUALITY OF OUR DIMENSION LUMBER IS FAR TOO GOOD FOR FRAMING PURPOSES. SAVED FULLY $100.00 ON A CARLOAD.

Hamilton, Ohio.

Sears, Roebuck and Co., Chicago, Ill.

Dear Sirs:—I received the lumber from you and found everything very satisfactory. I am highly pleased with my purchase. My contractor says that he has not at any time seen such fine lumber. If I can influence anyone to buy from you I shall do so. My carpenter tells me that he could not build a house with the same kind of material and buy the material in Hamilton for less than a 25 per cent advance over the price of my house. I can speak most highly of the material. Very truly yours,

H. KNIGHTON.

SEARS, ROEBUCK AND CO.  **CHICAGO, ILLINOIS**

BARN No. 14

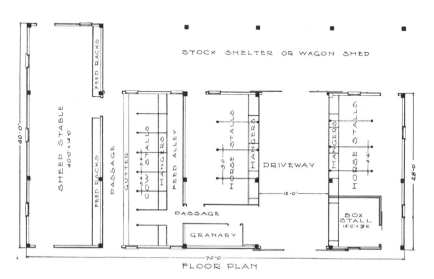

STOCK SHELTER OR WAGON SHED

SHEEP STABLE 40-0"x14-0"

FEED RACKS

FEED RACKS

PASSAGE

GUTTER

COW STALLS 3-6"x3-6"

MANGERS

FEED ALLEY

HORSE STALLS 5-0"

MANGERS

DRIVEWAY

13-0"

MANGERS

HORSE STALLS 4-6"

PASSAGE

GRANARY

BOX STALL 14-0"x9-6"

40-0"

28-0"

70-0"

FLOOR PLAN

—106—

$962.00

For $962.00 we will furnish all the material to build this Barn, consisting of Rough Lumber, Heavy Framing Timbers, Plank Flooring, Prepared Roofing, Sash, Hardware and Paint, Hay Carrier, Track and Rope.

By allowing a fair price for labor and concrete blocks, which we do not furnish, this barn can be built for about $1,300.00, including all material and labor.

For Our Offer of Free Plans See Page 3.

THIS barn is 40 feet wide and 70 feet long; 28 feet of the width and 56 feet of the length is used for horses and cattle, providing accommodations for eight horses and seven cows; also a box stall and grain room; 14x40 feet is left in one space and may be used for a sheep shed or for young stock. In addition to this, there is a space of 12x56 feet which is partly enclosed and will make an excellent cattle shed, or it may be utilized for the storage of farm implements.

This barn is constructed in the most substantial way and makes a practical barn at a moderate cost. Our specifications call for a heavy 3½-ply Red Slate Prepared Roofing guaranteed to last twelve years. Looks far better than shingles.

As will be seen from the floor plan the barn has a 12-foot driveway with doors high enough to admit a full load of hay so that the barn may be filled from the inside. A hay door is, however, also provided at one end, through which hay may be taken in with the carrier.

The barn is built on a concrete block foundation and all feed alley floors and driveway floors are made of cement. We furnish plank floors for the horse and cattle stalls.

SEARS, ROEBUCK AND CO.  **CHICAGO, ILLINOIS**

BARN No. 12

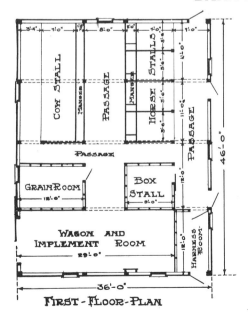

FIRST FLOOR PLAN

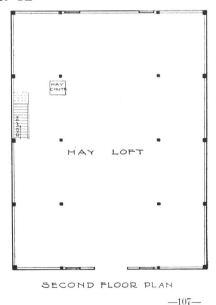

SECOND FLOOR PLAN

—107—

$651.00

For $651.00 we will furnish all the material to build this large Barn 36x46 feet, consisting of Rough Lumber, Framing Timbers, Plank Flooring, Roofing, Hardware, Sash and Paint, Hay Carrier Track and Rope.

By allowing a fair price for labor and concrete blocks, which we do not furnish, this barn can be built for about $900.00, including all material and labor.

For Our Offer of Free Plans See Page 3.

BARN No. 12 is 36 feet wide, 46 feet long and 14 feet high to the eaves. By reference to the ground floor plan it will be seen that provision is made for four horse stalls, one box stall, a harness room, grain room and about seven head of cattle. This leaves a space of 12 feet wide by 29 feet across one end of the barn for machinery or farm implements. The construction of this building is what is known as the Plank Frame style, that is, the timber, posts and girders are all built up out of 2-inch planks. This style of construction is coming into favor rapidly with all practical builders, as it has the advantage of cheapness and increased strength combined. The roof is of the gambrel type, self supporting, and offering no interference or obstruction to the hay carrier.

The materials we specify for this building are all first class. For the roof we furnish three-ply Red Slate Prepared Roofing which we guarantee to wear twelve years. It is easily put on and makes a better appearance than shingles.

We furnish sufficient paint for two-coat work for all the exterior woodwork, any color desired.

The barn is placed on a concrete block foundation and all passages and driveways have cement floors, while all stalls have 2-inch plank floors.

SEARS, ROEBUCK AND CO.  **CHICAGO, ILLINOIS**

A BRICK MANTEL, WOOD MANTEL OR CONSOLE MAKES THE MODERN HOME COMPLETE

Write for our Special Catalog of Mantels and Consoles and make your selection from the large half-tone illustrations shown therein. We offer a full line of red pressed brick mantels in all the modern styles and effects. Our solid oak mantels include large massive designs in full quarter sawed patterns and small cheap plain sawed bases for bedrooms, with all sizes and styles ranging between these extremes. They are finished in golden, antique and natural shades, polished and rubbed, or mission, weathered and Early English finishes. We also offer mantels painted white to be enameled, and any of our designs can be made in birch finished in imitation mahogany. Don't fail to get our Special Catalog of Mantels and Consoles before closing the contract for your modern home. It will be easier to have the mantel or console put in while the house is being finished than to order it later and put it in after the rooms are decorated. Write us a postal card or a letter today and say, "Send me your latest Mantel Catalog." We will mail it to you at once, free and postpaid.

$41⁰⁰ Palace Car Finish $41⁵⁰ Parlor Console

Full Quarter Sawed Oak, Hand Rubbed, Luster Polish | Rich Birch, Mahogany Finish, Hand Rubbed, Piano Polish

Console No. 35.

This console is 7 feet 6½ inches high by 5 feet wide. French plate bevel mirror, 54 inches high by 34 inches wide. Veneered columns, 5 inches in diameter. Shipping weight, 415 pounds. Prices, delivered on the cars at the works in Ohio.

No. 61C205 Quarter Sawed Golden Oak Console, polished, with French plate mirror.....................$41.00

No. 61C206 Rich Birch, Mahogany Finish Console, complete with French plate mirror...................... 41.50

Coal and Gas Fireplaces

Prices Delivered on the Cars at the Foundry in Ohio.

Sunbeam Grand Open Fireplace Mantel Grate

Made of heavy castings reinforced with extra thick firebrick lining. The front frame and summer piece are furnished in oxidized copper finish.

No. 61C3230 Open Fireplace Mantel Grate No. 128 is 30¼ inches high and 24½ inches wide, with 20-inch fire opening. Shipping weight, 210 pounds.
    Price $10.94

No. 61C3231 Open Fireplace Mantel Grate No. 128B is 30¼ inches high and 30½ inches wide, with 24-inch fire opening. Shipping weight, 250 pounds.
    Price $12.97

No. 128 With Summer Front.

Acme Colonial Open Gas Log Grate

This complete outfit is ready to be placed in position and connected with gas supply pipe. The top lining has adjustable dampers opening a draft to carry off the products of combustion.

No. 61C3252 Acme Colonial Gas Log Grate Outfit No. 26. Consists of an oxidized copper plated cast iron frame, 30¼ inches high and 24½ inches wide, with a fire opening 20 inches wide. The lower guard is cast iron and the guard rail is solid brass. The terra cotta gas logs are 16 inches long. Shipping weight, 95 pounds.
    Price $9.33

No. 61C3253 Gas Log Outfit No. 26B. The exact same style grate, measuring 30¼ inches high by 30½ inches wide, with a 24-inch fire opening and 18-inch gas logs. Shipping weight, 110 pounds.
    Price $10.25

No. 26 Gas Log Grate.

These two grates shown above are samples selected from our full line illustrated in our Special Mantel Catalog. We also show portable basket grates, brass and iron andirons, brass fire tools, fire screens and gas logs.

$17⁴⁰ Colonial Base, Three $17⁴⁰ Coats White

Mantel Base No. 807.

This Colonial base is 5 feet high to the surface of the shelf and full 5 feet extreme width. The fluted columns are 5 inches in diameter. The box, of which the shelf is the top surface, is 13 inches high. Total projection into the room is 11½ inches. Tile opening is 42 inches wide by 42 inches high, requiring a tile hearth 24 inches wide, extending the full width of the mantel. Profile, 2½ inches. Painted three coats white, ready to receive final coat. Shipping weight, 150 pounds. Price, delivered on the cars at the works in Ohio.

No. 61C410 Close Grained White Wood Mantel Base only. Price.....................................$17.40

For tile for the facing and hearth see page 109.

SEARS, ROEBUCK AND CO. —108— **CHICAGO, ILLINOIS**

Art Tile for Fireplace Facings and Hearths

Delivered on the Cars at the Tile Works in Ohio.

Persian De Luxe Mantel Tile. A discovery in tile glazing and colors. Beautiful rich dark oxbloods, deep chocolates, dark greens and mottled green. A renaissance of ancient tile beauty. A lost art restored. Furnished 6x2 inches with a 3-inch hearth border unless other sizes are desired. We can furnish them in all other standard sizes and half sizes when ordered. Price in barrel lots, 30 cents per square foot.

No. 61C3213 Set, complete, for a mantel opening 36x36 inches, with a hearth 60 inches long by 18 inches deep. Shipping weight, 80 pounds. Price......................**$3.76**

No. 61C3214 Set, complete, for a mantel opening 39x42 inches, with a hearth 60 inches long by 21 inches deep. Shipping weight, 106 pounds. Price......................**$4.87**

No. 61C3215 Set, complete, for a mantel opening 42x42 inches, with a hearth 60 inches long by 24 inches deep. Shipping weight, 116 pounds. Price......................**$5.50**

Satin or Matte Finish Mantel Tile. This modern soft satin finish enameling is much favored by architects, decorators and home art designers. Dark greens, dark olives, browns, chocolates, buffs, cream, dark tans, light tans, mottled cream and tan, cream and green, tan and green, and chocolate and green. Furnished 6x2 inches with a 3-inch hearth border unless other sizes are ordered. We can furnish them in all other standard sizes and half sizes when desired. Price in barrel lots, 27 cents per square foot.

No. 61C3216 Set, complete, for a mantel woodwork opening 36x36 inches, with a hearth 60 inches long by 18 inches deep. Shipping weight, 80 pounds. Price......**$3.40**

No. 61C3217 Set, complete, for a mantel woodwork opening 39x42 inches, with a hearth 60 inches long by 21 inches deep. Shipping weight, 106 pounds. Price......**$4.40**

No. 61C3218 Set, complete, for a mantel woodwork opening 42x42 inches, with a hearth 60 inches long by 24 inches deep. Shipping weight, 116 pounds. Price......**$4.98**

Brilliant Glazed Tile in beautiful blends and mottles. These are the tiles most popular for mantel facings and hearths. We furnish them in white and in the most brilliant enamel glazes, in all colors, tints and shades. This tile will always be furnished 6x1½ inches with 3-inch border unless other sizes are ordered. We can always furnish them in the other standard sizes and half sizes when desired. Price in barrel lots, 22½ cents per square foot.

No. 61C3220 Set, complete, for a mantel woodwork opening 36x36 inches, with a hearth 60 inches long by 18 inches deep. Shipping weight, 80 pounds. Price......**$2.94**

No. 61C3221 Set, complete, for a mantel woodwork opening 39x42 inches, with a hearth 60 inches long by 21 inches deep. Shipping weight, 106 pounds. Price......**$3.78**

No. 61C3222 Set, complete, for a mantel woodwork opening 42x42 inches, with a hearth 60 inches long by 24 inches deep. Shipping weight, 116 pounds. Price......**$4.23**

Mission Finish or Dull Brick Finish Unglazed Encaustic Mantel Tile. A wonderfully strong semi-vitreous, unglazed tile, furnished only in a dull dark brick red or a beautiful smooth brick dull buff color. Mission Mantel Tile will be furnished 6x2 and 3x2 inches with 3-inch border. Price in barrel lots, 18 cents per square foot.

No. 61C3226 Set, complete, for a mantel woodwork opening 36x36 inches, with a hearth 60 inches long by 18 inches deep. Shipping weight, 80 pounds. Price......**$2.28**

No. 61C3227 Set, complete, for a mantel woodwork opening 39x42 inches, with a hearth 60 inches long by 21 inches deep. Shipping weight, 106 pounds. Price......**$3.00**

No. 61C3228 Set, complete, for a mantel woodwork opening 42x42 inches, with a hearth 60 inches long by 24 inches deep. Shipping weight, 116 pounds. Price......**$3.37**

PURE WHITE TILE FOR THE BATHROOM FLOOR AND WALLS

This tile is made of clay and burned in a kiln at an intense heat until it is vitreous. The most sanitary, durable and beautiful treatment for bathrooms. A tile floor lasts forever. It is non-absorbent and as hard as glass. Moisture and dirt are easily wiped off the surface with a cloth and no scrubbing is necessary.

We are the originators of selling this material direct to the user. We offer you your first opportunity to secure floor tile and wall tile at any price. The associations of tile manufacturers and tile layers have heretofore controlled both the production and the distribution of tiles and have made it impossible for a home owner or a contractor to buy tile. They have forced all tile users to contract with them for the work complete and have made large profits on both the tile and on the work of laying it. Now that we have placed this material on the open market there is no longer any reason why every modern home should not have a fully tiled bathroom, kitchen, vestibule and porch floor. There is nothing better for the bathroom than a pure white floor of hexagonal tiles and for the walls, white glazed tile with sanitary cove base and neat cap. If colors are wanted they can be had to suit almost any taste or color scheme. White wall tile is made usually in 6x2-inch and 6x3-inch sizes, but we can furnish all other standard sizes if wanted.

No. 61C3546 Plain White Wall Tile. (Caps and bases extra.) Price, per square foot....................**22½c**

No. 61C3500 Plain White 1-Inch Hexagon Floor Tile. Price, per square foot........................**16c**

Send us a diagram of your bathroom showing the location of the doors and windows and tell us how high you want the wainscot and we will advise you just what the total cost will be, including the cap and base with corner angles and door stops. If you want to use plain wall tile without cap or base, you can send for the number of square feet you want at the above price and we will be glad to fill your order.

Write for our Tile Book and learn how to lay tile so that you can do the work yourself.

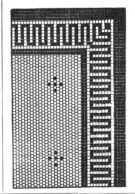

Beautiful Ceramic Tile Floor Patterns in Colors 16 Cents AND UP

16 Cents Per Square Foot and Up.

In our Special Tile Book we show many color plates of tile floor designs. We offer a large variety of these designs suitable for any and all rooms of any size.

We maintain that a properly laid ceramic mosaic floor is the most durable material ever produced for this purpose, and we will be sustained by any high class architect, builder or contractor. Ceramic mosaics are of hard, dense, non-porous, unglazed porcelain, burned with a heat of 3,000 degrees. They are absolutely fireproof, as hard as adamant, will not absorb moisture of any kind, and make the cleanest, most sanitary aseptic flooring known. Tile floors are extremely easy to keep clean. They are simply mopped up with clean water and soap. Scrubbing is rarely necessary. Sand soap should be used, and the more the floor is used and cleaned, the more beautiful it becomes.

Don't forget that floor tiles made from clay were in use 2,000 years before the inventors of substitutes were born, and they will be in use 2,000 years after the substitutes have rotted and decayed or have been thrown away as worthless.

Send us your order with a rough sketch of the floor to be tiled. Our Tile Color Book shows a beautiful assortment of tile designs to help you make your selection. Write us a postal card or a letter and ask for our Special Tile Color Book. It will be sent to you immediately on receipt of your request, free and postpaid.

Warm Air Furnaces for Modern Homes

When ordering your Modern Home do not overlook the prices quoted on Warm Air Heating Plants. We can make you the same proportionate saving on a furnace, registers and fittings as we can on the material to build the house. You will find our prices quoted at the foot of each page throughout this book.

Our Special Furnace Catalog gives detailed descriptions of these wonderful heaters. Learn how furnaces can be installed in old as well as new houses and read convincing letters from satisfied customers who have been enjoying the comforts of a well heated and ventilated home. Write and ask for our Special Furnace Catalog. It will be mailed to you at once, free and postpaid.

A BATTERY OF THREE WARM AIR GENERATORS OF UNSURPASSED EFFICIENCY

ACME HUMMER	ACME TROPIC	ACME UNIVERSAL

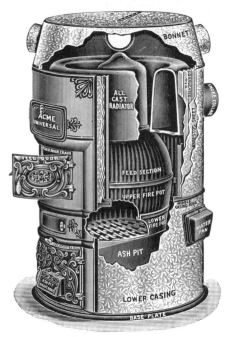

Made in Five Sizes.

For soft (bituminous) coal or wood. We offer this Acme Hummer Heating and Ventilating Furnace with broad top fire pot for soft coal or wood, as the best furnace on the market for the price. It has an extra large combustion chamber, making it a perfect soft coal burner and a quick heater. Wherever we specify in this book, "Warm Air Heating Plant for Soft Coal," we have based our price on this furnace.

Made in Five Sizes.

For hard (anthracite) coal or coke. We offer this Acme Tropic Heating and Ventilating Furnace with circular steel radiator for hard coal or coke, as the quickest and most efficient furnace to be had. The castings are heavy and well made and the circular radiator is so constructed that the greatest amount of heat is obtained from coal consumed. We guarantee this furnace to be the equal of any other furnace made. Wherever we specify "Warm Air Heating Plant for Hard Coal" in this book, we have based our price on this furnace.

Made in Five Sizes.

For hard or soft coal. This is a new furnace built along the lines of our popular Acme Tropic, but equipped with an all cast iron radiator for burning soft as well as hard coal. There is considerable demand for a furnace of this type with a cast radiator and our Acme Universal has been prepared especially to fill this want. We will be very glad to figure on this furnace for your Modern Home in place of the Hummer or Tropic. The cost will be a few dollars more, but it will be well worth the difference to have a furnace in which you can burn hard or soft coal at pleasure.

REMEMBER, we can heat any house anywhere, whether it be a cottage, residence, flat building, schoolhouse or church, and guarantee to heat the building to 70 degrees in the coldest weather.

STEAM AND HOT WATER HEATING PLANTS

We ship without delay, for we keep at all times a complete line of boilers and radiators at our factory, and a full stock of valves, pipe, fittings, etc., at our Chicago store.

Our estimates are free, and our prices include everything needed, excepting the labor of installation. We can save you an immense amount of money on any kind of a heating plant installed under our binding guarantee of absolute satisfaction or money returned.

We furnish with each order received a complete working drawing showing in a very plain and simple manner the way the plant is to be installed. With the aid of this drawing, any man at all handy with tools will experience no trouble in installing these plants and you not only save considerable money on the material furnished, but avoid the expense of installation as well. You take no chances, as we assume all risk.

Write for our 48-page free book Modern Heating Systems. We quote a few heating materials on this page just to show you how much we can save you, but if you need a heating plant don't fail to write at once for our free special catalog, "Modern Heating Systems," a splendid book of 48 pages, telling you everything you want to know and quoting the lowest possible prices. We also send you a printed diagram sheet which you can easily fill out, showing the style and size of your house, and on receipt of this rough plan we furnish you with a complete itemized estimate, showing exactly what the entire plant will cost you. We charge you nothing for this valuable service.

HERCULES BOILERS, $29.60

Our Hercules Boilers Are Superior to Any Other Line of Heaters, Either Round or Sectional, That Are on the Market Today

The Hercules Steam and Hot Water Boilers quoted on this page are of the vertical sectional type and have all the advantages of the round boiler, such as compact fire pot and simplicity of construction, while they also have the superior advantages of the sectional boilers, such as long fire travel, increased heating surface and the correct proportions between the grate and the heating surface. The fire pot is deep and the return flues ample, so it will do its work economically and with the least attention. It will carry coal enough to maintain perfect combustion for twelve hours with ordinary care and attention. For hot water heating this heater is superior to any small heater on the market, as it has a perfect interior circulation, and this is also especially advantageous for steam, as the steam is more easily generated and is quickly separated from the water, so that the water is not carried up into the pipes with the steam. The heater is thoroughly tested before leaving the works and is made up and shipped in two parts; base and grates in one and the sections in the other, which makes it easy to erect. Its compact form enables it to be carried into a building as easily as a radiator.

The steam boiler is furnished complete with all steam trimmings, such as steam gauge, water gauge, and damper regulator and safety valve. These are not necessary with a hot water boiler. All boilers are furnished complete with firing tools, such as poker, hoe and flue brush.

Hercules Steam and Hot Water Boilers are shipped from factory in Western Pennsylvania.

WRITE FOR CATALOG OF HEATING PLANTS.

No. 42C2013

Comfort Steam or Hot Water Three-Column Radiators

SHIPPED FROM FACTORY IN WESTERN PENNSYLVANIA.

OUR RADIATORS ARE OF THE LATEST IMPROVED DESIGN, AND THE PATTERN CANNOT FAIL TO BE ACCEPTABLE TO ANY OF OUR CUSTOMERS, AS IT IS NEAT AND ATTRACTIVE

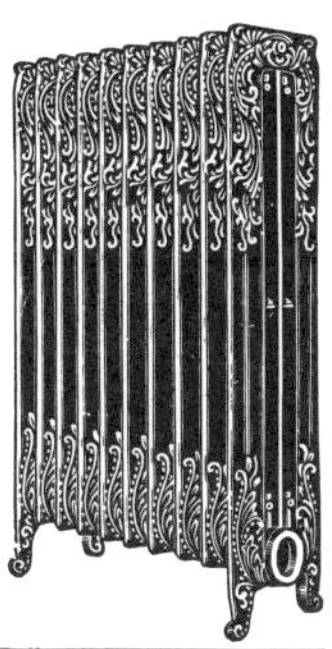

Our hot water radiators are constructed to hold a pint of water to a foot of radiating surface. This enables us to have a wider space between the sections for the circulation of the air and enables the radiators to do more effective work in giving out heat, both by radiation and contact with the air. **The castings are made of the finest grade of gray iron** of uniform thickness, with corrugated heating surface, and are free from all flaws and pinholes. The castings are tested to 70 pounds pressure before leaving our factory. We can furnish radiators in any number of sections desired.

When ordering be sure to state whether you want radiators for steam or hot water.

STEAM RADIATORS ARE TAPPED AS FOLLOWS:	HOT WATER RADIATORS ARE TAPPED AS FOLLOWS:
Up to 24 feet.........................1 -inch supply	Up to 50 feet.........................1 -inch feed and return
24 feet to 50 feet................1¼-inch supply	50 feet to 75 feet...............1¼-inch feed and return
50 feet to 100 feet...............1½-inch supply	Over 75 feet......................1½-inch feed and return
Over 100 feet.......................2 -inch supply	

LIST OF SIZES, THREE-COLUMN RADIATORS.

No. of Sections	Length, Inches	HEATING SURFACE—SQUARE FEET					
		45-Inch Height. 6 Square Feet per Section	38-Inch Height. 5 Square Feet per Section	32-Inch Height. 4½ Square Feet per Section	26-Inch Height. 3¾ Square Feet per Section	23-Inch Height. 3¼ Square Feet per Section	20-Inch Height. 2¾ Square Feet per Section
2	5	12	10	9	7½	6½	5½
3	7½	18	15	13½	11¼	9¾	8¼
4	10	24	20	18	15	13	11
5	12½	30	25	22½	18¾	16¼	13¾
6	15	36	30	27	22½	19½	16½
7	17½	42	35	31½	26¼	22¾	19¼
8	20	48	40	36	30	26	22
9	22½	54	45	40½	33¾	29¼	24¾
10	25	60	50	45	37½	32½	27½
11	27½	66	55	49½	41¼	35¾	30¼
12	30	72	60	54	45	39	33
No. 42C2054 Price, per square foot, steam.................		18c	18c	21c	23c	25c	26c
No. 42C2055 Price, per square foot, hot water.................		19c	19c	22c	24c	25½c	27c

No.	Size of Fire Pot, Inches	Size of Smoke Pipe, In.	H'ght, Inches	Floor Space, Including Smoke Box	Flow and Return	Rating, Water	Rating, Steam	Price, Water	Price, Steam
134	13x11	7	47	22x22 in.	2-2	300	150	$29.60	$ 37.75
135	13x14	7	47	22x26 in.	2-2	400	225	40.45	48.75
136	13x17	7	47	22x30 in.	2-2	525	300	50.00	58.00
175	17x17	8	58	26x28 in.	2-2½	650	400	55.00	63.00
176	17x22	8	58	26x32 in.	2-2½	900	500	73.00	81.00
177	17x27	8	58	26x36 in.	3-2½	1,050	600	83.00	91.00
178	17x31	8	58	26x40 in.	3-2½	1,250	700	99.00	107.00

Write for our Special Heating Catalog for complete information on steam and hot water boilers ranging from 125 to 5,000 square feet of heating surface.

MODERN PLUMBING

IS THE NAME OF OUR LATEST PLUMBING CATALOG, WHICH TELLS IN DETAIL ALL ABOUT OUR COMPLETE LINE OF MODERN UP TO DATE PLUMBING FIXTURES, AND ALSO ILLUSTRATES AND DESCRIBES THE MATERIAL NECESSARY FOR INSTALLING THEM. WRITE FOR IT.

Stop and consider what it means to you to be able to save from $50.00 to $75.00 on a bathroom outfit or from $100.00 to $150.00 on the complete plumbing for your house. Don't you think it would pay you to investigate our material, to write for a copy of our Plumbing Catalog and see for yourself whether or not this statement is true? There is no doubt but that we can make you a large saving in the plumbing for your building, and, further, there is no doubt but that we can furnish you with a very high grade of plumbing material.

Our reason for being able to list such high grade material at exceedingly low prices is that we manufacture all of our own plumbing fixtures in our own factory, which is equipped with modern labor saving machinery. In this factory we employ the highest skilled mechanics, who are expert in their work of making high grade plumbing goods. Because of the care taken in manufacturing, we can sell our plumbing fixtures under the binding guarantee that they will be absolutely satisfactory in every way, and that our enameled goods, such as sinks, lavatories, etc., are made of the highest grade of gray iron throughout, carefully enameled with the best grade of white enamel which will not chip, flake or crack.

Our closet bowls, earthenware tanks, etc., are made of A1 vitreous earthenware heavily glazed and will be found to be equal to any on the market.

It is not necessary that you employ an expert plumber to install our bathroom outfits, kitchen sinks or other fixtures, inasmuch as we can furnish all of this material threaded for iron pipe, when so ordered, and we send detailed instructions and working plans so simple that anyone at all handy with pipe fitting tools can do the work of installing them.

Carefully examine the outfit we list on this page, and then stop and consider whether or not you want to pay your local plumber or some other concern a fabulous profit for your plumbing material. As stated above, we manufacture all our own plumbing fixtures, and the cost to you is the actual cost of manufacture with but our small profit added.

Don't fail to write for our latest Plumbing Catalog; a postal card will bring it. It will mean a saving to you.

Perfection Bathroom Outfit

$37 95

Just to give you an example of the enormous saving we can make you in high grade plumbing goods, we list and illustrate our Perfection Bathroom Outfit, consisting of a tub, lavatory and closet complete, with supply and waste pipes to the floor and wall, as shown in the illustration.

The tub is made of the highest grade of cast iron throughout, carefully enameled on the inside and painted on the outside. It has a large roll rim and is equipped with a No. 4½ Fuller bath cock, bath supplies, and connected waste and overflow. The bath cock, supply, waste and overflow pipes are made of brass, heavily nickel plated, and with ordinary care will last a lifetime.

The lavatory is also made of the highest grade of gray cast iron and is enameled inside and outside to the bottom of the apron. It is also equipped with brass supply and waste pipes, trap, and hot and cold indexed basin cocks, all of which are heavily nickel plated.

The closet is a low down closet combination. The tank and seat are made of golden oak, highly polished, and the bowl is of vitreous earthenware of the siphonic washdown type, heavily glazed inside and outside.

Compare this outfit with bathroom outfits offered by other houses handling plumbing goods, who advertise in magazines and elsewhere, and you will find that they cannot furnish you with an outfit of the same quality and manufacture as the one listed below at anywhere near the price we ask for it.

Ask your local plumber what he would charge for an outfit of this kind and see what he tells you. He will probably say that he can install the outfit in your home for $150.00. Stop and consider what this means. It means that he is making an enormous profit on the bathroom outfit he is selling you, and is also making a large profit on the material for installing it and the actual work of putting it in.

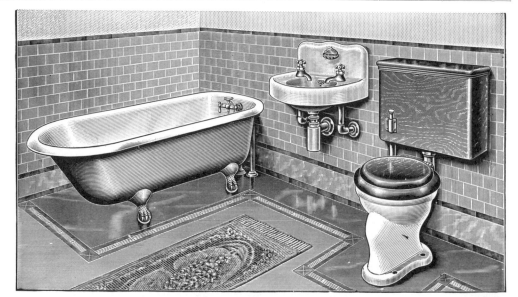

No. 42C9214 Perfection Bathroom Outfit, complete. Price..................$37.95

For the convenience of our customers we can furnish the above outfit with all fittings threaded for iron pipe connections at an extra charge of $1.50.

PAINTS AND FINISHING MATERIALS

WHITE LEAD, VARNISHES, STAINS, SHELLAC, FILLERS AND KALSOMINE

We handle everything needed for interior and exterior finishing and can save you about half on any painting or finishing material. Every item is guaranteed to be of the highest quality. Our low prices are the result of manufacturing nearly all material ourselves in the best equipped and most up to date paint factory in the country.

Seroco Guaranteed
Ready Mixed House Paint
$1.18 Per Gallon
In 1-Gallon Cans.

Price Still Lower in Larger Quantities

Our Seroco Ready Mixed House Paint cannot be beat for wear, covering capacity and finish. We guarantee it not to peel, blister, chalk nor rub off.

Seroco Guaranteed
Weatherproof Mineral Barn Paint
84c Per Gallon
In 1-Gallon Cans.

Price Still Lower in Larger Quantities

Our Weatherproof Mineral Barn Paint is the best mineral paint that can be made. We will match it for wear, finish, gloss and covering capacity against any mineral paint on the market, no matter what the price.

Color Sample Book and "How to Paint"
Two Splendid Books FREE on Request

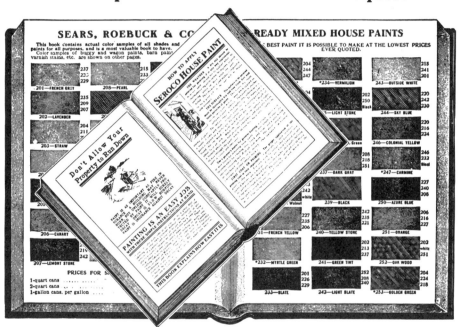

Our Seroco Ready Mixed House Paint and our Weatherproof Mineral Barn, Roof and Fence Paints are guaranteed not to peel, blister, rub nor chalk. You simply cannot afford to lose this protection by buying your paints elsewhere. If you are thinking of painting now or in the near future send to us at once for our two free books, our Color Sample Book in which we show you the actual colors of all of our various paints, and our useful little booklet entitled "How to Paint," telling you just how to do any job of painting. Send for these books at once and let us save you from $5.00 to $25.00 on the material you need for your paint job, show you how to do the work yourself, save the expense of a regular painter and protect yourself against loss and disappointment by our binding guarantee.

Ask today for our Color Sample Book of Paints and "How to Paint" Book and we will send both books by return mail free of cost.

We Name Here a Few of Our Prices

Our Paint Color Sample Book quotes lowest prices on everything. Send for it today.

	Price
Extra Light Hard Oil Finish. Per gallon	$1.20
No. 1 Light Hard Oil Finish. Per gallon	.95
Seroco Cabinet Finish. A splendid varnish for interior woodwork. Per gallon	1.30
Seroco Interior Spar Varnish. A better varnish for interior woodwork cannot be made. Per gallon	1.75
Seroco Durable Floor Varnish. Nothing better on the market. Your money back if you can find a better wearing varnish. Per gallon	1.70
Pure Orange Shellac in denatured alcohol. Per gallon	1.40
Pure White Shellac in denatured alcohol. Per gallon	1.55
Oil Stains. Per gallon	1.24
Varnish Stains. Per gallon	1.30
Best Prepared Floor Wax. Per pound	.28
Paste Wood Filler. 5-pound cans. Per pound	.06
Kalsomine or Wall Coating. Best and easiest working. Nothing to compare with it for finish and covering power. Per package (will cover from 500 to 600 square feet)	.24

We handle a full line of Paint, Varnish, Kalsomine, Whitewash, Wire and Waxing Brushes, and other Painters' Tools. See our prices before you place your order.

Just a Few of the Many Letters We Receive Daily

READ WHAT OUR CUSTOMERS SAY. Look at the photographic reproductions of 22 of the 1,340 houses built from our plans and with our materials (see opposite page). We have satisfied the builders and saved them money. We can do the same for you. No one takes any risk when doing business with us. **WE GUARANTEE** to save you money and satisfy you in every respect.

$3,500.00 House for $2,540.00.

No. 7 is a picture of our Modern Home No. 114, built at Halifax, Pa., by Mr. N. E. Noblet. He says: "All your lumber and materials are excellent. I have saved from $250.00 to $300.00 by dealing with you. Many think my home cost $3,500.00. I built it complete for $2,540.01." For floor plans and full description see page 51.

Saved 35 Per Cent.

No. 15 is a picture of our Modern Home No. 118, with some alterations, built at Terrell, Texas, by Mr. Josephus Autrey. He says: "The amount saved by buying the mill work, hardware and plumbing material of you is about 35 per cent, or at least one-third." For floor plans and full description see page 11.

Saved $225.00.

No. 17 is a picture of our Modern Home No. 147, with some alterations, built at Mandon, N. D., by Mr. Arthur Witherow. He says: "The material was fine, and I could not wish better. I saved about $225.00 after paying freight." For floor plans and full description see page 88.

One Sells Another.

No. 4 is a picture of our Modern Home No. 111, built at Ossining, N. Y., by Mr. Geo. E. Twiggar. The same house has been built at Havre de Grace, Md., by Mr. J. H. Howlett. These houses can always be put up at a big saving. The materials will be found to be far better than can be secured in the local market. For floor plans and full description see page 46.

Saved $800.00.

No. 13 is a picture of our Modern Home No. 132, built at Colorado City, Colo., by Mr. John M. Clear. He says: "I have saved on my order about $800.00, and the quality of the material far surpasses any that is being furnished here." For floor plans and full description see page 10.

Saved 50 Per Cent.

No. 19 is a picture of our Modern Home No. 114, with some alterations, built at Rochelle Park, N. J., by Mr. John C. Johnson. He says: "I could not have obtained the same material here for less than about twice the amount I paid you, which was between $800.00 and $900.00. All transactions have been attended to promptly and fairly in every respect." For floor plans and full description see page 51.

"The Talk of the Town."

No. 2 is a picture of our Modern Home No. 132, built at Paxton, Ill. The builder states that it is the "talk of the town" on account of its imposing appearance and the extra good quality of the materials with which it is constructed. None of the local concerns would compete for the job when shown our figure. For floor plans and full description see page 10.

A Double House for the Price of a Single One.

No. 11 is a picture of a Modern Home built at Concord, N. H., by Mr. P. T. Gulley. He says: "I found the prices of your mill work and building hardware so reasonable that I built a large double house and made a large saving."

Saved $500.00.

No. 16 is a picture of our Bungalow No. 151, built at Greeley, Colo., by Mr. W. H. Segier. He says: "The material is the best in any house in Greeley, a town of 10,000 population. I saved $500.00." For floor plans and full description see page 32.

"A Big Saving."

No. 10 is a picture of our Modern Home No. 111, built at Havre de Grace, Md., by Mr. J. H. Howlett. He says: "I am sending you a photo of my house built from your plans and with your material at a big saving to me. Materials are far better than I could have secured in our city at a much higher price." For floor plans and full description see page 46.

"Splendid Modern Dwelling."

No. 6 is a picture of our Modern Home No. 123, built at Ossining, N. Y., by Mr. Samuel T. Davis, who tells us that it gives him much pleasure to send us a photograph of the splendid modern dwelling which has been constructed according to our plans and with our material. The owners are evidently proud of this house, as their own pictures are shown in connection with it. For floor plans and full description see page 24.

Saved $200.00.

No. 5 is a picture of our Modern Home No 167, built at Grafton, Mass., by Mr. D. S. Chase. He says: "The lumber and finishing material are much better than I could have gotten here. My contractor tells me that I have saved nearly $200.00 on the whole." For floor plans and full description see page 47.

Saved $500.00.

No. 20 is a picture of our Modern Home No. 24, built at York, Neb., by Mr. J. P. Berck. He says: "We were more than satisfied with everything received. There was not even a piece of poor material in the entire bill. We have saved fully $500.00 on this building." For floor plans and full description see page 68.

Beyond Expectations.

No. 14 is a picture of our Modern Home No. 114, built at Monongahela, Pa., by D. F. Addison. He says: "I found everything beyond my expectations and thank you for the honest way you treated me in the deal." For floor plans and full description see page 51.

Never Saw Such Good Doors.

No. 8 is a picture of our Modern Home No. 132, built at Douglas, Wyo., by Mr. G. N. Doyle. He says: "The material was satisfactory in every way, especially the inside finish. I never saw as fine oak doors." For floor plans and full description see page 10.

"Admired by All."

No. 18 is a picture of our Modern Home No. 119, built at Baltimore, Md., by Dr. S. R. Wantz. He says: "I am well pleased with the material, which is admired by all. Many thanks for the way you treated me." For floor plans and full description see page 42.

"Way Down South."

No. 3 is a picture of our Modern Home No. 119, built at Martinez, Ga., by Mr. R. T. Lyle. As can easily be seen, it is a roomy and substantial structure, and altogether a house very popular with our customers who demand something above the ordinary. For floor plans and full description see page 42.

Saved 30 Per Cent.

No. 12 is a picture of our Modern Home No. 123, built at Bay Shore, L. I., N. Y., by Mr. S. J. Smith. He says: "The red oak trim is the prettiest lot of mill work I ever saw. I saved at least 30 per cent on the material." For floor plans and full description see page 24.

Saved Nearly $400.00.

No. 1 is a picture of our Modern Home No. 146, built at New Rochelle, N. Y. The builder for good reasons of his own does not wish his name to be printed, but states that he saved between $300.00 and $400.00 on this house and got a very fine quality of lumber and mill work. For floor plans and full description see page 4.

Saved $300.00.

No. 9 is a picture of our Modern Home No. 114, built at Norwalk, Ohio, by Mr. F. D. Cronk. He says: "I have the nicest house in town for the money and saved about $300.00 by dealing with you." For floor plans and full description see page 51.

Saved $300.00.

No. 21 is a picture of two of our Modern Homes No. 133, built at Barrington, Ill., by Messrs. Halverson & Groff. They say: "The material ordered from you was better than first class if that could be possible. We saved $150.00 on each house." For floor plans and full description see page 49.

"One of the Best."

No. 22 is a picture of our Modern Home No. 118, built at Fenton, Iowa, by Mr. Philip Weisbrod. He says: "Your material cannot be praised high enough for quality. My house is one of the best in this community." For floor plans and full description see page 11.

BUILT BY OUR CUSTOMERS AT A BIG SAVING

Exact Reproductions of Photographs of Houses Built From Our Free Plans and With Our Materials. See Builders' Letters on Opposite Page.

This house is shown in colors on the front cover of the book. Interior views in colors are shown on inside front and back cover pages and on back cover.

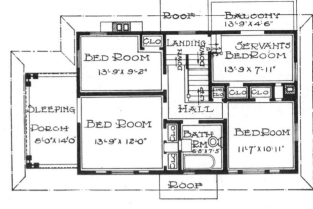

Furnishings shown in colored illustrations not included in the price.

SECOND FLOOR PLAN

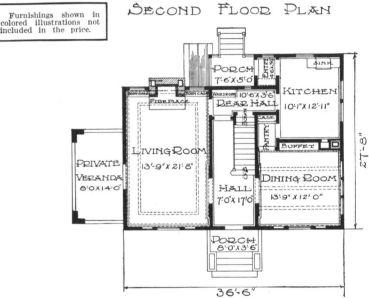

FIRST FLOOR PLAN

$1,564⁰⁰

MODERN HOME No. 230

For $1,564.00 we will furnish all the material to build this Seven-Room House, consisting of Lumber, Lath, Shingles, Ceiling, Siding, Flooring, Finishing Lumber, Building Paper, Pipe, Gutter, Sash Weights, Buffet, Cabinet Work, Hardware, Mosaic Tile Flooring, Brick Mantel and Painting Material. NO EXTRAS outside of plumbing and heating, as we guarantee enough material at the above price to build this house according to our plans.

By allowing a fair price for labor, cement, brick and plaster, which we do not furnish, this house can be built for about $3,275.00, including all material and labor.

FOR OUR OFFER OF FREE PLANS SEE PAGE 3.

THIS modern home was designed by one of Chicago's leading architects. It is up to date, attractive and well arranged for good ventilation and convenience. It contains many features found only in the more expensive houses and, considering the low cost at which this house can be built, it makes a fine investment as well as a desirable home.

First Floor.

Front door is made of oak, 1¾ inches thick, Craftsman style, glazed with plate glass. French doors, glazed with heavy plate glass, between veranda and living room, between living room and hall and between hall and dining room. Compound oak doors between living room and rear hall, and between pantry and living room. Oak floors and trim in living room, dining room and hall. Large open brick fireplace in living room. Dining room contains a modern built-in buffet, also plate rail and beamed ceiling. Kitchen, rear hall and pantry have yellow pine doors and trim, and maple floors. Built-in wardrobe in rear hall. Built-in cupboard in pantry. Open stairway of oak to second floor.

Built on a concrete block foundation, veneered with brick from the grade to the first floor joists. Framing timbers are of the best quality yellow pine. Cedar shingle roof. Clear cypress siding.

Excavated basement with cement floor under entire house and under veranda, and is 7 feet from floor to joists. First floor is 9 feet 3 inches from floor to ceiling. Second floor, 8 feet 9 inches from floor to ceiling.

Stain and paint for exterior; varnish and wood filler for interior included in above price.

This house requires either a corner lot 50 feet wide or inside lot 75 feet wide to set off building properly.

Complete Warm Air Heating Plant, for soft coal, extra	$101.52
Complete Warm Air Heating Plant, for hard coal, extra	103.53
Complete Hot Water Heating Plant, extra	288.19
Complete Steam Heating Plant, extra	241.95
Complete Plumbing Outfit, extra	125.27

Second Floor.

Open stairway to hall on second floor from which the bathroom, linen closet or any of the bedrooms may be entered. French doors glazed with heavy plate glass open onto sleeping porch, also on balcony in the rear. Two mirror doors glazed with heavy plate glass mirrors in front bedroom at the left. Tile floor in bathroom. Medicine cabinet built in the bathroom. Clothes chute to the basement is situated between the two bedrooms at the right. Yellow pine floors in the hall, closets and all four bedrooms. Two-panel birch doors with trim to match used for entire second floor. Open stairway to attic. Attic is floored.

(116)